Inverness, Black Isle and Affric
40 Favourite Walks

published by
pocket mountains ltd
The Old Church, Annanside, Moffat,
Dumfries and Galloway DG10 9HB
www.pocketmountains.com

ISBN: 978-1-907025-34-1

Text copyright © Paul and Helen Webster

Photography copyright © Paul and Helen Webster

The right of Paul and Helen Webster to be identified as the Authors of this work has been asserted by them in accordance with the Copyright, Designs and Patents Act 1988

A catalogue record for this book is available from the British Library

Contains Ordnance Survey data © Crown copyright and database right 2012, supported by out of copyright mapping from 1945-1961

Printed in Poland

Introduction

Thanks to Nessie, its legendary resident monster, Loch Ness is one of the best known places in Scotland. Situated on the Great Glen Fault, the immense depth of the loch – some 230m – means that it holds nearly twice as much fresh water as all the lakes of England and Wales combined.

For lovers of the outdoors, the loch is merely the centrepiece of an area offering an amazing variety of walking. The 40 walks in this book include canalside towpaths, loch shore rambles, explorations of ancient forest and coastal cliffs, as well as the city streets of Inverness. North of Loch Ness are the great Caledonian pinewoods of Glen Affric, backed by magnificent mountains and reckoned by many to be the finest glen in the country. At the meeting point of the River Ness and the Beauly Firth sits the vibrant Highland capital, Inverness, and a quick hop across the Kessock Bridge leads to the fertile Black Isle with its coastal walks, dolphins and red kites.

How to use this guide

Most of the 40 walks in this book can be completed in half a day or less, leaving plenty of time for another walk or a visit to a café, attraction, distillery, historic site or boat trip. Inverness is a useful transport hub, and most of the walks can be accessed by public transport with a little planning and some flexibility with times.

Whilst some of the walks are on good paths and a few are waymarked, requiring only basic navigation, many are also in fairly remote areas where help can be far away. It is always recommended to take the relevant OS map and compass and to know how to use them. Waterproof clothing, decent footwear and a map should be taken on all but the shortest or urban routes, whilst additional hillwalking equipment and map-reading skills are needed for the wildest and hilliest routes. Midges can sometimes be a problem in the summer months on still, damp days, particularly in Glen Affric, though they dislike strong sun or a breeze. If you are unlucky, cover up, wear light clothing and experiment with repellents. Avon *Skin so Soft* is used by many locals to prevent bites, whilst a midge-hood can help on a very still evening if you don't mind being immersed in mesh.

Transport, access and dogs

Inverness is well connected to the rest of the UK, with the mainline rail link to the south as well as good coach services and an airport. The Wick/Kyle of Lochalsh rail lines have stations at Dingwall, Muir of Ord and Beauly, whilst most of the walks in the book can be reached from Inverness using local bus services. Where a walk can be reached by public transport, it is flagged up in the text. Timetables can be found in tourist information centres throughout the region and from Traveline Scotland.

Scotland has some of the most progressive access laws in Europe following the passing of the Land Reform (Scotland) Act 2003. This gives walkers a right of access over most land away from residential buildings. With these rights come responsibilities which are set out in the Scottish Outdoor Access Code. Basically these require walkers to respect other land users and to act responsibly, especially on farmed and grazing land. In particular, dogs should be kept under tight control during the spring and early summer to prevent disturbance to groundnesting birds. They should also be kept away from livestock with young at all times. Stag stalking takes place out on the hills between 1 July and 20 October, but should not cause a problem with the routes in this guide.

History

The bronze age burial cairns and standing stones at Clava Cairns, just east of Inverness, date back 4000 years and provide spectacular evidence of the long history of human occupation in the area. A couple of millennia later saw the construction of 'vitrified' forts on many of the region's hilltops. These are visited on several of the walks, such as the Craig Phadrig and Ord Hill routes that overlook Inverness and one of the finer examples at Knockfarrel near Dingwall. They were built with no lime or cement, the stones having been fused together by heating to a great temperature – though exactly how this was achieved remains a mystery.

The Jacobite rebellions are perhaps the historic period with which the area is most associated. The initial abortive rebellions in support of the exiled King James VII in 1689 and 1715 were soon crushed and, in the aftermath, the government began an attempt to subdue the Highlands, now seen as a major threat. General Wade began the construction of a series of forts in the Highlands along the line of the Great Glen, at Fort William, Fort Augustus and Fort George on the coast east of Inverness, together with a new network of roads. In spite of Wade's work, Bonnie Prince Charlie – the grandson of James VII – landed in Moidart in 1745 to lead the second major Jacobite uprising. This time the government army was outmanoeuvred as his forces took Edinburgh and Carlisle on their way south. At Derby, with nothing to bar their route on to London, Charles and his advisors were misled by a spy who claimed that a huge army was lying in wait. Retreat followed and, with momentum lost and his men exhausted, the army was crushed at Culloden near Inverness in 1746.

In the aftermath, the Highlands were ruthlessly repressed. The bearing of arms was outlawed, as was wearing tartan and written Gaelic. The clan system began to collapse and, as the Industrial Revolution in the south was creating a massive demand for wool, the chiefs began to turf out their people to make way for sheep. The Highland Clearances had begun and saw many areas emptied of people; potato famine and industrialisation were also drawing or driving people away from the Highlands to the cities down south or emigration to the New World. The Caledonian Canal was built in the hope that by securing a safe coast to coast shipping route, economic development might begin to provide employment. Whilst never fulfilling its potential at the time, the canal has since become a major tourist attraction. The biggest attraction, however, remains Loch Ness itself, largely due to the legend of Nessie. First photographed in 1933, stories had long circulated of a prehistoric monster with a long neck and humped back that lived in the deep waters of the loch. Despite scientific expeditions using sonar, boats and submarines, no conclusive proof of the monster has been forthcoming.

Wildlife

Whilst Nessie proves to be elusive, the area has much to offer the amateur bird- or wildlife watcher. Red deer can be found in large numbers around Glen Affric, with the autumn rut being particularly spectacular. Red squirrels and pine martens are also present, but it is the dolphins of the Moray Firth that are the biggest draw. The school of around 190 dolphins resident here are regularly spotted off Chanonry Point on the Black Isle. Such is their popularity that they even have their own 'groupies'; regular watchers who can usually be found at the point during the summer armed with scopes and binoculars, providing a wonderful source of information about the latest habits of these lovable creatures. Boat trips from Cromarty and Avoch provide the opportunity to spot the pods from the sea and you may also catch a

glimpse of otters, ospreys, seals, harbour porpoises, basking sharks and minke whales, as well as a variety of seabirds.

Golden eagles can often be seen soaring on the thermals, though it requires careful observation to avoid confusing them with buzzards. The Slavonian Grebes on Loch Ruthven are a strong attraction for keen twitchers, but it is the red kites of the Black Isle that are probably the region's best known avian inhabitant, easily identified by their distinctive forked tail. A heart-warming success story, these impressive birds were reintroduced under a programme which began in 1989. Today, there are approximately 50 pairs in the area. Persecution continues to deplete their numbers, however, and studies suggest the Black Isle population might now have topped 300 pairs if it were not for illegal poisoning.

Otters are prevalent in much of the area, although they are elusive creatures best spotted in the water. Curiously, one of the best places to spy them is from the road end in the South Kessock area of Inverness (see page 88), where regular wildlife spotters wait patiently from the comfort of their cars, armed with binoculars. The Black Water, featured in the Rogie Falls and Silverbridge routes (see pages 62-64), offers a chance to watch for leaping salmon as they make their way upstream to spawn in the late summer and autumn. The surrounding forests are said to be a stronghold of the native Scottish wildcat, though sightings are very rare.

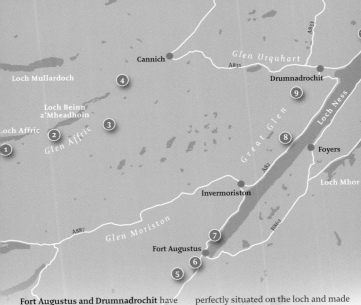

Fort Augustus and Drumnadrochit have long been popular centres for visitors on the north shores of Loch Ness. Fort Augustus grew up around a stronghold built in the era of the Jacobite rebellions, one of a line of forts running along the Great Glen. Later the construction of the Caledonian Canal through the same glen saw a picturesque flight of locks built which became the very heart of the village. Today these still provide a busy spectacle in the summer months as leisure craft of all sizes jostle with larger boats whilst kayakers portage their boats past the staircase. Drumnadrochit counters with an attraction of its own – the ruins of Urquhart Castle being

perfectly situated on the loch and made familiar through countless postcards. The village is also home to two exhibition centres dedicated to the loch's most famous resident – Nessie.

The land rises steeply from the loch for much of its length, with only Glen Moriston and Glen Urquhart providing easy passage northwards. The latter leads through to Cannich, itself the gateway to perhaps the most beautiful glen in all Scotland, Glen Affric. The Scots pines of the ancient Caledonian forest still stand proudly here, backed by magnificent mountains – this is the epitome of Highland scenery and a wonderful refuge for wildlife.

Glen Affric and North Loch Ness

Loch Affric

Distance 18km **Time** 6 hours 30
Terrain good tracks and paths in a very
wild area, including a burn crossing which
would be hazardous in spate; navigation
skills, map and hillwalking kit essential
Maps OS Explorer 414 and 415
Access Ross's Minibuses operate a service
(5) from Inverness to Glen Affric three
days per week in summer

The longest walk in this book, the circuit
around Loch Affric passes through remote
and wild countryside far from help. It is,
however, a gem – the loch is fringed by
remnants of the ancient Caledonian
pinewood and makes a perfect foreground
to the grand mountains all around.

Start from the car park (parking charge)
at the end of the road up Glen Affric and

begin by walking on the track which
continues where the public road ends. At
the fork, bear right to head uphill, passing
the No Entry sign which refers to vehicles.
Birchwoods eventually give way to Scots
pines as the route skirts the lower part of
Loch Affric.

Don't be tempted to take the track
which curves down to the cottage on the
lochside; instead keep right to follow a
path above the fence. As the trees thin,
the prominent peak of Sgurr na Lapaich
can be seen ahead. Go through the gate in
the deer fence – fencing is one of a
number of strategies employed to try to
aid natural regeneration of the forest.
Many of the pines here are direct
descendants of trees that grew up after
the end of the last ice age about 10,000
years ago. Whilst the ground is relatively

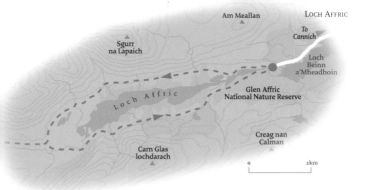

infertile and unattractive for farming, it has long been a source of wood – with commercial timber being felled as early as 1560 when it was used for bridge building in Inverness. Continued felling along with the growth in the importance of sheep during the 19th century further reduced the size of the Caledonian forest. Once the last of the wolves had been killed, there were no natural predators and, aided by protection from the large sporting estates, the deer population exploded during Victorian times. It is the unnaturally high numbers of deer that has been partly responsible for the fact that only one percent of the original Caledonian forest now remains in Scotland. Efforts to reverse this trend have been made by the Forestry Commission for Scotland and charities such as Trees for Life – you may well encounter tree planting and fence-repairing volunteers on this route.

The track passes some fine pine specimens known as Granny Pines due to their age – it is said that these same trees could have sheltered Bonnie Prince Charlie when hiding in the glen from government troops.

Cross the Allt Coire Leachavie, leaving behind the pines to head over more open moorland. Boulders usually allow a dry crossing of the Allt Coulavie, but this could become dangerous or impassable in spate. On the far side the track continues, passing above Loch Coulavie. At a wider track, turn left (a right turn eventually leads you to the remote hostel at roadless Alltbeithe). This route soon passes picturesque Strawberry Cottage, a climbing club hut, where it crosses a bridge over the River Affric.

Turn left along the riverbank until you rejoin a track which provides great views on the walk back above the south side of the loch. Eventually the route enters a fenced area of forest and passes Loch Salach a Ghiublais. The views are particularly beautiful on the later stretches; remain on the main track after a bridge and pass above the narrow lower section of Loch Affric, eventually turning left at a fork to return to the car park.

◀ Snow on Sgurr na Lapaich above Loch Affric

9

River Affric and Am Meallan

Distance **1.5km** Time **45 mins**
Terrain **waymarked paths, rocky in places
with steps** Map **OS Explorer 415**
Access **Ross's Minibuses operate a service
(5) from Inverness to Glen Affric three
days per week in summer**

**Though short, this little route has
everything one could want from a
Highland leg-stretcher – idyllic scenery,
magnificent pines, a tumbling river and
views of a stunning loch backed by
high mountains.**

After the long and winding drive up
Glen Affric, the public road comes to an
end at an expansive car park (parking
charge), testament to the popularity of
what is often described as the most
beautiful glen in Scotland. Here there are
picnic tables, toilets and information
boards about the local walks. Both the
waymarked walks are short, and this walk
combines them in a figure of eight. Start
by following the blue waymarked path,
dropping downhill with good views of
Loch Beinn a'Mheadhoin. As the path
meanders through the trees, it runs close
to the River Affric where it forces a route
through a small gorge.

As the route bears right, it keeps near

the river. Steps have been constructed to ease the going across rocky ground as the route passes a small waterfall. Keep following the waymarkers as the path aims to the right, leading uphill past a bench with a fabulous outlook over the glen before dropping back to the car park. The second part of the walk follows the white waymarkers to Am Meallan – the path starting opposite the road leading into the car park. Take either option at the fork as the walk loops from here. The short climb up to the highest point is

rewarded with a truly classic view out over Loch Affric into the wild upper glen, backed by some of the highest mountains in the northwest Highlands.

A memorial here commemorates the foresters and conservationists who have worked to help restore and regenerate the ancient Caledonian forest, particularly HM Steven, the former Professor of Forestry at Aberdeen University and President of the Society of Foresters. Continue round the loop to return to the car park.

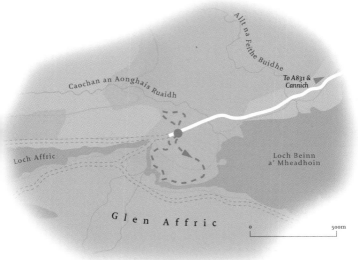

◀ Looking over Loch Affric to the mountains at the head of the glen

Plodda Falls and the Tweedmouth Walk

Distance 2.5km **Time** 1 hour
Terrain clear, waymarked paths; some
steep sections near the falls
Map OS Explorer 415 **Access** no public
transport; nearest bus stop is at Tomich
with infrequent services from Inverness
and Beauly

Plodda Falls is the highest and most
spectacular waterfall in Scotland that
can be approached closely and easily.
You can gaze down at the rushing water
from a cantilevered platform that hangs
over the 40m-high falls. This circular
walk takes in the best viewpoints, as
well as exploring the forest of mighty
Douglas Firs.

The parking for Plodda Falls is signed
from the picturesque village of Tomich;
reaching it involves driving several
kilometres along a bumpy forest track. At
the car park (parking charge), there is an
information board with the walk marked;
this route follows the green waymarkers

of the Tweedmouth Walk. A shorter walk,
waymarked in white, can be taken to just
see the falls if time isn't on your side.

Follow the wide track (SP Tweedmouth
Walk), heading down into the forest for
around 300m, keeping an eye out for a
waymarked path on the left. Take this but
almost immediately fork right, following
the green markers. The path now winds
down through a variety of tall Douglas Fir
and European larch trees, some of the
tallest in Scotland. These trees were
mainly planted between 1895 and 1900;
the Douglas Firs, being strong, tall and
straight, were highly prized for use as
ships' masts. Trees from here were used
to replace the masts on Captain Scott's
ship *Discovery* during its refurbishment;
the ship is now berthed in Dundee.

The path emerges on a track just west of
Plodda Cottage. Whilst the route
described here turns left, it is possible to
detour along the old carriage drive to the
right for about 2km to see the ruins of

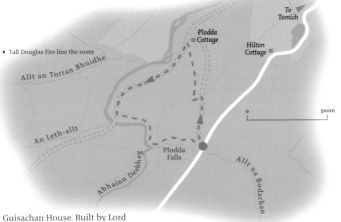

◄ Tall Douglas Firs line the route

To Tomich

Plodda Cottage

Hilton Cottage

Allt an Torran Bhuidhe

An Leth-allt

Plodda Falls

Abhainn Deabhag

Allt na Bodachan

0   500m

Guisachan House. Built by Lord Tweedmouth, this replaced a much earlier one destroyed by government troops following the 1745 rebellion. As well as being responsible for the development of the forest, Lord Tweedmouth built the model village of Tomich – allegedly so he didn't have to look out over his tenants and their crofts. The house was later used as a training centre before being purchased in 1939 by the owner of nearby Hilton Lodge, Lady Islington, who objected to seeing residents of the house swimming in Hilton Loch. The roof was removed and the house gradually succumbed to the elements, becoming a ruinous shell.

Back on the route, follow the track until a marker indicates a path off to the left just before the track reaches the river at a ford which makes a good picnic stop. Take this path, climbing through the trees to reveal a first distant glimpse of Plodda

Falls. At the next path junction, detour to the right down to an excellent viewpoint near the base of the falls. Here, the water plunges vertically for around 40m into a twisting gorge; the force of water usually showers anyone standing here in a fine mist or a deluge of spray, depending on the level of water.

Return to the path, continuing steeply uphill to reach the top of the falls. Lord Tweedmouth erected a fine metal bridge over the falls in 1880 as an impressive showpiece for guests. Despite being restored, the original bridge became unsafe and Forest Enterprise have now built a viewing platform that juts out directly over the lip of the falls. A head for heights is needed for the dizzying view down the falls to the floor of the gorge. From here, it is only a short stroll uphill to return to the car park.

13

Dog Falls and Coire Loch

Distance 6km **Time** 2 hours
Terrain forest paths; steep and rough in
places **Map** OS Explorer 415 **Access** Ross's
Minibuses operate a service (5) from
Inverness to Glen Affric three days per
week in summer

Step back in time on this hike through
remnants of the ancient Caledonian
pinewoods that once carpeted much of
Scotland. Surely one of the most beautiful
forest walks in Scotland, the route gives
views into a dramatic gorge, and climbs
through the trees to reach a beautiful
hidden lochan.

Dog Falls car park (parking charge) is
well signed, approximately 6km up the
glen from Cannich (turn right when the

road forks). Here, you'll find picnic tables
overlooking the foaming River Affric as
well as toilets and an information board.
This route combines all three waymarked
trails to explore the best of the Glen Affric
forests in a relatively short outing.

Begin by heading downstream,
following the red waymarkers; the path
soon climbs up and crosses the road. Keep
to the path as it traverses the hillside,
keeping walkers off the narrow, winding
road below. Once each year, this section of
road is transformed into a seething mass
of racing cyclists competing in the
Highland Cross – a gruelling coast to coast
duathlon that ends with a mad cycle down
to the Beauly Firth.

At the next junction, detour to the right

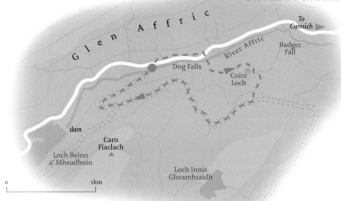

to view the falls, heading down and across the road to visit a small viewing area. The raging water is squeezed through a narrow gorge and over the Dog Falls – spectacular for their power and setting rather than any great height. Return back to the path on the far side of the road and continue to the right; it soon leads down and crosses the road again to reach a long wooden suspension bridge high over the river.

The trail now climbs through the pinewoods with some impressive ancient specimens and an abundance of bird and wildlife. Ignore the red trail which leaves to the right and instead remain on the yellow waymarked route winding through the forest. After a short but steep climb, a beautiful view over Coire Loch is reached with a handy felled trunk of pine making a natural bench.

The waymarked path continues down the far side of the crag – down steep steps in places – to reach the shore of the loch. Dragonflies can be seen dancing across the surface of the water in the summer months, adding flashes of jade to the greenery. Follow the path around the lochan before a wider track is reached. Turn right here, following the route until a T-junction with a larger track. Again turn right, passing a number of information posts about this special forest and the creatures that make their home here. Ignore a path to the right (SP Dog Falls) and continue to a clear junction where the red route turns right to return to the car park. If you have the energy, it is worth turning left to follow white markers for 500m until a marked viewpoint off to the right gives a view over Loch Beinn a'Mheadhoin towards the rugged mountains at the head of the glen. From here retrace your steps back down the track and continue to cross the bridge to reach the car park at the start.

◀ Viewpoint over Coire Loch

Oich Swing Bridge to Fort Augustus

Distance 8km Time **2 hours 30**
Terrain **level canal towpath**
Map **OS Explorer 400**
Access **regular bus (19, 919) from Inverness and Fort William stops at Swing Bridge House at Aberchalder**

Take the bus from Fort Augustus to the beautiful Oich Bridge before walking back along the Caledonian Canal to watch the boats navigating the flight of locks that lead down to Loch Ness.

Alight from the bus at the Aberchalder Swing Bridge over the Caledonian Canal near Bridge of Oich; on the north side of the canal where there is a small car park. Before beginning the walk along the towpath it is worth detouring to look at Oich Bridge, a beautiful old suspension bridge over the River Oich which runs

close to the canal. Now maintained by Historic Scotland the double-cantilevered bridge was built by James Drudge in 1854 and no longer carries the busy A82 so is a great spot to admire the surroundings. To begin the walk, head back over the canal and then turn left along the southeast bank, passing the Bridge House Tea Garden. The route then crosses back over the canal at Cullochy Lock and from this point continues along the northwest bank for the whole walk to Fort Augustus.

The Caledonian Canal is an impressive feat of engineering. Built under the direction of Thomas Telford and William Jessop, it was Telford's passionate hope that the canal would invigorate the Highland economy at a time when mass emigration, the Highland Clearances, the potato famine and industrialisation had

robbed the area of its economy and there seemed little prospect of local jobs. One of the ironies of the ambitious project was that Irish navvies had to be brought in to plug a gap in the workforce, and by the time the entire canal opened in 1847 the smaller craft which the canal had been designed for had given way to larger steamships. Today, however, it has undergone a revival as a popular coast to coast route for tourist boats, cruisers and canoeists. The Great Glen Way, a long-distance footpath from Fort William to Inverness, follows sections of the towpath and has become very popular in recent years.

As the towpath continues through pleasant woodland there are glimpses of the River Oich on the left; at one point the cliffs of Creag Torr Dhuinn can be seen. After another 3km Kytra Lock is reached, a picturesque spot where a bench allows walkers to watch any boats negotiating the lock, backed by the lockkeeper's cottage and surrounding hills.

The canal eventually broadens into a series of wider pools and another 3km of steady walking brings you to the first of the flight of locks that leads down through Fort Augustus. You can follow the canal all the way to its exit into Loch Ness; Fort Augustus itself is well worth exploring with a range of canalside pubs, restaurants, shops and a canal museum.

◀ Locks of the Caledonian Canal at Fort Augustus

River Oich meander

Distance 6km **Time** 2 hours
Terrain almost flat tracks and riverside
path **Map** OS Explorer 400 **Access** bus (19,
919) from Fort William and Inverness to
Fort Augustus, then 1km walk (follow
signs for Auchteraw and River Walk)

**This easy going walk on forest tracks leads
through impressive Scots pines – a
favourite spot for red squirrels – before
continuing along the banks of the stately
River Oich.**

It is possible to drive to the start or walk
an extra 1km each way from the main car
park in Fort Augustus; either way, take the
A82 towards Inverness and then the steep
left-hand turn up Bunoich Brae (SP
Auchteraw). Pass a first car park and keep
following the signs for Auchteraw,

keeping to the left to reach the Forestry
Commission car park.

From here plunge into the trees by taking
the path signed for the River Walk. Keep to
the right and follow the yellow waymarkers
as the path heads through birch trees. At a
track bear left to pass through a plantation
of tall firs. The long straight section of track
is lined by some impressive Scots pines.
The Scots pine is the only pine tree native
to Northern Europe; it normally lives for
between 150 and 300 years, though some
'grannies' (as the oldest, most gnarled
specimens are affectionately known) have
reached over 700 years old. This mighty
pine has been adopted as Scotland's
national tree and supports a massive array
of wildlife, being the bedrock of the ancient
Caledonian forest.

◄ Watch for red squirrels among the tall pines

Allt na Fearna

Fort Augustus

Caledonian Canal

A82

Auchteraw

Torr a'Choiltreich

Loch Uanagan

River Oich

Kytra Lock

To Invergarry

A82

0   1km

Continue on the track, ignoring a path to the left, cross a small bridge and pass under power cables. After eventually passing a track on the right, take the left-hand waymarked path to reach the riverbank. Follow the river downstream. The river is popular with salmon fishermen and has a number of slower running pools from which trout can also be caught. Local ghillies keep the banks clear and a bench makes a fine picnic spot.

The towpath of the Caledonian Canal is soon seen on the far side of the river; the two watercourses run alongside each other on this stretch. After crossing a burn, follow the path as it leads away from the riverbank to the left to return to the car park.

19

Allt na Criche

Distance **2.5km** Time **1 hour**
Terrain **waymarked paths and forest track;
one steep section** Map OS Explorer 416
Access **no public transport to start**

**This short waymarked woodland
walk climbs past an attractive waterfall
and gives good views over Loch Ness.
The return leg follows the Great Glen Way.**

Some 2km north of Fort Augustus off
the A82 is the Forestry Commission car
park for Allt na Criche. Start from the back
of the car park and follow the white
waymarked path. This climbs up beside
the Allt na Criche burn, passing a waterfall
before turning away from the burn and
climbing more steeply. Still climbing
steadily the path heads through mixed
woodland of silver birch and pines which
can be teeming with small birds at many
times of year. In the late summer and

autumn the forest floor here is
particularly good for spotting fungi. After
a period of wet weather the rate of growth
and variety of species is amazing, with
new toadstools literally appearing
overnight. As with all fungi care should
be taken about handling them as many
are poisonous – there are sometimes
guided fungi walks in the area during the
season where experts can help identify
the varieties.

The route levels off briefly before again
climbing uphill, with stone steps leading
to a forestry track. Turn left along the
track which gives some great views of
Loch Ness below. After a short while Fort
Augustus comes into sight at the head of
the loch. The town grew up around its
position on the mid point of the Great
Glen route and was also a religious
centre with the Abbot of Iona

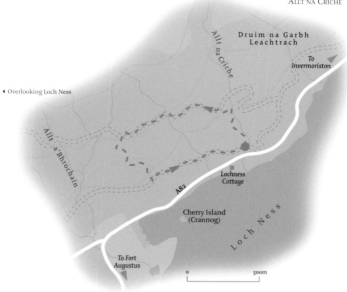

‹ Overlooking Loch Ness

establishing a church here in the 6th century – the impressive abbey buildings now provide holiday accommodation. In the aftermath of the 1715 Jacobite rising a fort was built here by General Wade. The fort was named after the second son of King George II, the notorious Prince William Augustus, Duke of Cumberland, who led the victorious government troops at the Battle of Culloden. The Duke earned the moniker 'Butcher Cumberland' due to atrocities inflicted on the defeated Highlanders – he reportedly ordered his troops to give no quarter and in the period after the rebellion, 'sympathetic' villages were

burned and livestock confiscated across the region.

Look out for a marker post indicating a path off to the left after a right-hand bend in the track. Follow this path downhill through the pines, passing a couple of seats before emerging on a track. This forms part of the Great Glen Way which runs for 100km between Fort William and Inverness and is a popular long-distance walking route. Some people combine it with the West Highland Way to link the cities of Glasgow and Inverness in a longer trek. This walk, however, simply returns to the car park by turning left along the Great Glen Way.

Meall Fuar-mhonaidh

Distance 9km **Time** 5 hours
Terrain moorland hill path; rocky, eroded
and boggy in places **Map** OS Explorer 416
Access no public transport to start

**Climb to the summit of the most
prominent hill above Loch Ness, a rough
hillwalk rewarded with superb views.**

At 699m, Meall Fuar-mhonaidh looks
impressive when viewed along Loch Ness
from Dores and other vantage points. It
provides a straightforward hillwalk but,
like any outing into the hills, does require
navigation skills and proper outdoor gear.

The route starts from the end of the
Bunloit road from Drumnadrochit – to
reach it follow signs towards the pottery.
After 6km (but before the pottery and
road end) there is a parking area on the

right-hand side. Start by walking further
along the road (SP hill footpath) but then
keep right where the road swings left over
the bridge to the pottery. The path
continues pleasantly beside the burn at
first, with the objective, Meall Fuar-
mhonaidh, seen directly ahead.

The path then leaves the burn to bear
right, soon going through two gates to
cross over a track; keep following the
signs. Climb through birch and hazel
woodland with an attractive burn on the
left. The gradient steepens for a time
before levelling out; go through another
gate in a fence. The woods soon begin
to thin as the path continues up onto
open moorland.

Looking back there is a first glimpse of
Loch Ness, though much more ascent is

needed to get the best views. The path curves slightly left and climbs a high stile over a deer fence to head up onto a ridge. Once on the ridge bear left along a clear path – the going does become much rougher underfoot and can be boggy in places. After passing a rocky crag a small dip leads to the final steeper climb to the summit area.

The cairn, which has been in view during the final stages, is not quite the highest point which is a short distance beyond, also marked with a cairn. From here, there is an excellent view along the length of the Great Glen to Ben Nevis as well as back down Loch Ness. The return is by the same outward climb – it's no hardship to retrace your steps with such a great view ahead.

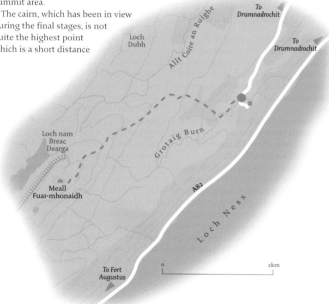

◀ Summit cairn of Meall Fuar-mhonaidh

23

Craigmonie and the Falls of Divach

Distance 10km **Time** 3 hours 30
Terrain waymarked forest footpaths and
minor roads; can be very muddy in winter
Map OS Explorer 416 **Access** bus (19, 919)
between Fort William and Inverness stops
at Drumnadrochit

**The fine views from the hilltop fort of
Craigmonie above Drumnadrochit reward
an initial climb; the walk continues to
reach the fine Falls of Divach.**

Drumnadrochit is a popular halt midway
along the north side of Loch Ness, with
nearby Urquhart Castle drawing visitors all
year round. The village provides welcome
facilities for walkers on the Great Glen Way
as well as boasting two competing Nessie
exhibitions. The best way to appreciate the
location by Loch Ness is to climb up to the
viewpoint on this walk. Start from the car
park in the centre of Drum, which houses
the tourist information centre and toilets.
Heading out from the car park, turn right
along the road, then right at a crossroads
(SP Craigmonie and Balmacaan) to follow
Pitkerrald Road. At a fork in the road
branch left to head gently uphill. Pass a
sign for Craigmonie to reach an old
information board on the right, beneath a
magnificent Giant Redwood tree. Our route
follows parts of both the red and green
waymarked trails. Bear right on an earth
path heading uphill, following red
waymarkers at first; very soon keep right
onto a lower, narrower path at a fork. The
route stays fairly near the fence.

Good views of Loch Ness are revealed
through the birch trees, and the path is
soon joined by another coming in from the
left. At a fork in the path bear right slightly
downhill, now following green
waymarkers as the path traverses the
flanks of Glen Urquhart. Keep a sharp ear
out for the sound of woodpeckers and red
squirrels which are often heard before they
are spotted; pine martens have also been
reported in this part of the woods. Stay on
the level path, ignoring a track to the left,
and cross a couple of small bridges before
the path swings left, heading steeply uphill

◄ Looking over
Drumnadrochit to
Loch Ness

to reach the Milton viewpoint (on the left). Here a seat provides a view over the settlement of Milton, named after the mills that produced the Glen Urquhart black and white checked tweed in the 1800s. Continue climbing until a crossroads of paths; go straight ahead here into the pines (green waymarker). At the next junction leave the green route and turn right to follow the red waymarkers along a track uphill beside a fence. Very soon turn left onto a path (red marker) heading to the brow of Craigmonie Crag.

Once the site of an iron age fort, Craigmonie (sometimes spelt Craig Mony) is named after a Viking prince who retreated here following a battle. Later the site is said to have been used for executions. Beyond the seat the path undulates past massive boulders and Scots pine trees. At a fork leave the red route to branch right downhill to the edge of the woodland, turning left along another path which runs along the inside edge of the woods. Stay on this path, ignoring two paths to the left, before bearing right to pass some old waterworks. Don't cross the stile here, instead remaining on the path which follows the left side of the fence through the woods, crossing a track at one

point. At a fork branch left, eventually passing through a gateway between a house and a watertank. Turn left towards the house to reach the track, then right to follow this, keeping left around a sharp bend (ignore the track off ahead) to reach a minor road. Head right along the road alongside the River Coiltie, soon crossing it on a bridge. The road then climbs steeply uphill; keep right at a fork, with good views over Drumnadrochit to the right, and continue to the small Falls of Divach car park. From here a signed path leads through woodland to a fenced viewpoint for the falls. To return to the village head all the way back along the road. At a road junction with a 30mph sign turn right, continuing along the road past the cottages of Lewiston until a sign for Drumnadrochit leads you to the left up a track. Take the fenced path which branches on the right; this eventually bears right and follows a field edge to the main A82 road. Turn left here for the short walk back to the car park.

25

The Old Coffin Road

Distance **4km** Time **1 hour 30**
Terrain **woodland paths; very steep and
muddy in parts** Map **OS Explorer 416**
Access **bus (19) between Fort William and
Inverness stops at the Clansman Hotel**

**Follow in the footsteps of the coffin
bearers of yesteryear on this airy walk
high above Loch Ness.**

This route starts from the Clansman
Hotel on the A82 on the north side of Loch
Ness where there is a popular café. Begin
from the north end of the car park beyond
the coach parking where there is an
information board about the woodland
trails. The broad path climbs into
Abriachan Woods, revealing fine glimpses
of Loch Ness through the trees as height is
gained. The gradient is steady and the path
was obviously well planned – it was once
used by funeral corteges to bring the

coffins of the deceased down from the
high crofts for burial. Keep climbing until
you see a dogleg sharply to the left – don't
take this path – it is the return route.
Instead carry on for a short distance before
turning right at a junction.

Soon there is a seat at a viewpoint on
the right, providing a good opportunity
to get the binoculars out to watch for
birds of prey – or perhaps just to catch
your breath.

The upper section of path can be muddy
at times; continue along it to reach a gate
and stile, leaving the woods behind for
more open countryside. Pass below the
house at Balchraggan before bearing left,
climbing up alongside it to reach a track.
Turn left here, ignoring the first track off to
the right but taking the second (SP Peat
Path and Carn na Leitire) which soon
climbs back into the trees. At one point,

◄ Rest spot on the Great Glen Way overlooking Loch Ness

there is a path off to the right which enables you to connect with the trails at Abriachan (see page 29) for those looking for a longer walk. Otherwise continue along the track to eventually reach a picnic table and signpost at another junction. Turn left here, following the path signed for the Loch Ness Clansman. This descends to reach a bench perched on the edge of a steep drop

down to Loch Ness – it gives wonderful open views over the loch and beyond.

The path now bears left to descend steeply – it is rough and rocky in places. Soon the outward route is rejoined at the junction passed earlier; keep heading downhill, passing round the sharp right-hand bend to eventually return to the start at the Clansman Hotel.

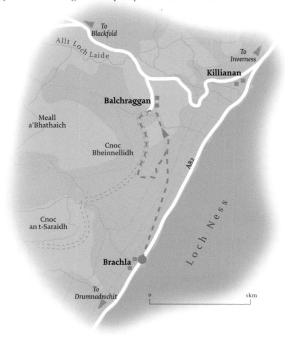

Abriachan Trails

Distance 8km **Time** 4 hours
Terrain good paths and tracks; some short
climbs **Map** OS Explorer 416
Access no public transport to start

**A treehouse, recreated bronze-age hut,
whisky still and hilltop summer sheiling
provide continual interest on this fine
walk around the forest and moorland path
network at Abriachan.**

Abriachan is an old crofting community
set in the hills above Loch Ness. Whilst the
population of the scattered settlement has
now dwindled to around 140 people, the
community came together in 1996 to
purchase an area of commercial forestry
with the aim of enhancing public access.
Since then the Abriachan Forest
Community Trust has slowly increased the
amount of native woodland and
constructed paths, educational and fitness
facilities, all helping to create employment.

The approach from the A82 running

along Loch Ness is steep and is signed
near the entrance to Abriachan Nursery.
If heading from the south, it is necessary
to use the turning area on the opposite
side of the road as the bend is too steep to
approach directly. Go left at a fork and
after passing Loch Laide turn left up the
signed forest track to reach the car park,
where there are picnic tables, toilets and
information about the forest and trails.
The route described here takes in most of
the features and varied habitats of this
high and exposed site.

Start by following the trail signed for
the 'wee treehouse' and Loch Laide. To
visit the treehouse, detour left at the
junction before returning to continue
along the path. Bear right at the next fork
and then left at a T-junction, staying on
the main path which curves left to visit a

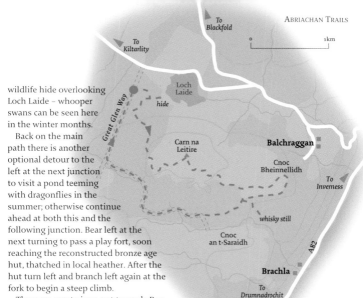

wildlife hide overlooking Loch Laide – whooper swans can be seen here in the winter months.

Back on the main path there is another optional detour to the left at the next junction to visit a pond teeming with dragonflies in the summer; otherwise continue ahead at both this and the following junction. Bear left at the next turning to pass a play fort, soon reaching the reconstructed bronze age hut, thatched in local heather. After the hut turn left and branch left again at the fork to begin a steep climb.

There are great views out towards Ben Wyvis from a bench that been beautifully carved from a tree trunk. At the junction turn left (SP Carn na Leitire). Head across the moorland, passing another carved bench and keeping left at the next junction for a detour to a wooden sculpture with a great view, before continuing across the moor to the small summit marked with a cairn where the views are even better. Turn left once more (SP Peat path, Balchraggan), passing a wooden sculpture here, and follow the sign to the sheiling. Sheilings were huts where folk would make their home in the summer months to look after their flocks on the high grazings. Made of turf, the sheiling provides good shelter if the

weather is poor. To continue, follow the path to reach a track and turn right. Stay on the track (SP Great Glen Way) – at one point there is an optional detour to the left to visit a reconstruction of a hidden whisky still where illicit spirit might have been distilled away from the prying eyes of the government's excise officers. Back on the main route, keep on until the Great Glen Way joins in from the left at a larger track. Keep right here, soon passing the highest point on this popular long-distance route. Ignore the signed path to the right, and after a gate pass a barn and the straight track eventually leads back to the car park at the start.

◀ Summer sheiling high above Loch Ness

Beauly Firth

Beauly

Inverness

A862

Strathglass

Glen Urquhart

Cannich

A831

Drumnadrochit

④

⑤

Loch
Duntelchaig

Loch
Ruthven

③

Loch Ness

Strathnairn

Great Glen

A82

②

① **Foyers**

Loch Mhor

Glen Moriston

A887

Invermoriston

A82

Fort Augustus

The impressive waterfalls at Foyers
ensured that the south side of Loch Ness
became an essential part of the Grand
Tour. The later building of the main A82
Fort William to Inverness road on the
north side has since led to this area
becoming a quiet backwater, neglected by
many visitors. The villages here are small
and undeveloped, spared the coachloads of
Nessie spotters, though Loch Ness' only
permanent Nessie hunter has been
resident in a van on the shores of the loch
near the Dores Inn for more than a decade.
This rural idyll is shaken once each year
when the RockNess festival springs to life,
a weekend that always brings surprises
with both the musical line-up and the
range of Highland weather.

Strath Nairn is notable for its many
smaller lochs; Loch Ruthven, in particular,
is well worth a visit as the breeding ground
for the rare but striking Slavonian Grebe.
The area is enclosed to the south by the
long barrier of the rolling Monadhliath
mountain range.

Dunlichity Kirk ▶

South Loch Ness

The Falls of Foyers

Distance 4km **Time** 1 hour 30
Terrain waymarked paths with some steep
sections and steps; minor road
Map OS Explorer 416 **Access** bus (16) from
Inverness to Foyers

The Falls of Foyers have been attracting
tourists since the early 18th century and
are still a major draw for visitors to the
south side of Loch Ness. This short but
spectacular walk follows the edge of the
gorge to a viewing area before exploring
the woodland and visiting Lower Foyers.

Waterfalls have always been popular
with sightseers and when the Scottish
Highlands first opened up to tourism the
Falls of Foyers quickly became established
as a fixture on any tour taking in the great
romantic sights. Rabbie Burns
immortalised the waterfall in a poem
penned in 1787; visitors would arrive by
horse or from across the loch by steamer.
Start from Upper Foyers where there is a
car park, shop and café. From here cross
the road and go through the left-hand
gate, signed for the Falls of Foyers.

The stepped path travels quickly
downhill to reach a superb viewpoint for
the main falls. The volume of water varies
greatly depending on recent weather.
Reduced to a trickle after a long dry spell,
in spate the falls truly thunder over the
62m drop, great consolation after a wet
week in the Highlands.

After the viewpoint, continue downhill,
ignoring a path to the right for now to
reach another viewing area. From here,
return to the junction and bear left along
a fenced path which skirts the edge of the
deep gorge. As the path drops through
the woodland, there is a fine view of the
lower falls which, whilst not so high,

◀ The bridges of Lower Foyers

enjoy a fine setting.
Look out for red
squirrels amongst
the trees, listening
for their distinctive
scratching rustle as
they scamper up and
down the trunks using their
sharp claws for gripping and
tails for balance.

Eventually the path emerges
at a gate with a hotel to the right;
turn left down the track, passing
several houses. When the road is
reached at a T-junction, turn left
to pass the medical centre and
continue downhill around a
bend to reach the lower bridge.
The east side of Lower Foyers is
dominated by the shell of a large
aluminium factory, built at the end of the
19th century after an early conservation
battle. The fight against its construction
pitted visitors against industrialists in a
battle still being repeated across the
Highlands today. Objectors to the plans
thought it would draw too much water
from the river, spoiling the falls and hence
reduce visitors to the village; the matter
was even raised in parliament, but the
factory eventually went ahead. Although it
closed in the 1960s, water is still drawn
from the river and used by the nearby
power station.

Cross the bridge and immediately turn
right onto a riverside footpath leading to

fishing huts on the banks of Loch Ness.
Bear left to follow the pebbly shore along
a faint path which eventually climbs
slightly left to follow a higher path
amongst the trees. This leads to a
memorial; from here continue through the
trees around the edge of a cemetery to
reach the access track. Follow this back
towards the houses of Lower Foyers, going
left when it meets a road and continuing
back to the bridge. From here retrace the
outward route back to the start. Halfway
up as the path swings right towards the
falls near the rim of the gorge it is possible
to take a more direct path up through the
trees to reach the café at the start.

33

Inverfarigaig and Foyers circuit

Distance 10.25km **Time** 4 hours
Terrain waymarked paths, rough and steep
in places; navigation skills and map needed
Map OS Explorer 416 **Access** bus (16) from
Inverness to Inverfarigaig or Foyers

**This varied circuit passes through mixed
woodland high above the south side of
Loch Ness to reach Foyers where you can
stop for a break and view the waterfalls
before returning closer to the lochside.**

Whilst the Falls of Foyers are worth a visit
in their own right, this route approaches
via a series of woodland paths, making the
village of Foyers with its shop, café and
hotel the half-way point. The route starts at
the Farigaig Forestry Commission car park
signed from the B852 at Inverfarigaig. There
are toilets and a small information centre
here. The route is waymarked in red to
Foyers and follows mostly blue
waymarkers for the return.

Start by heading up the path past the
information centre which climbs uphill
into the forest. Take the optional detour to

the right (SP Loch Ness viewpoint) if you
want to do a spot of Nessie spotting. This
part of the forest is also popular with roe
and sika deer so keep your eyes peeled;
stay on the meandering path as it returns
to the main red waymarked route and turn
right to continue uphill. The path soon
widens to become a track; keep left at a
first fork until the path reaches a second
fork. Here ignore the signed route to the
shore on the right but stay left to climb up
out of the trees onto heather moorland.

The route traverses the hillside at first;
keep a keen eye out for red markers on
trees and stones as the meandering path
can be difficult to spot as it dips into a pine
wood. Once out in more open ground the
route passes a number of rocky outcrops
with good views over Loch Ness.

Unseen below the route is Boleskine
House, home of Aleister Crowley between
1899 and 1913. As well as being an
enthusiastic mountaineer, Crowley was the
founder of his own brand of religious
philosophy and purchased Boleskine for its

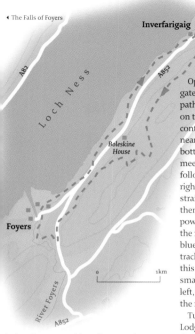

◀ The Falls of Foyers

Inverfarigaig

A82

A82

Loch Ness

A852

Boleskine
House

Foyers

River Foyers

A852

0 ————— 1km

Opposite the shop take the right-hand gate to view the Falls of Foyers. Follow the path to the two viewpoints and then keep on the signed path for Lower Foyers, continuing down a track when it emerges near the Foyers Bay House Hotel. At the bottom of the hill turn left when you meet the road, pass a medical centre and follow the road round a sharp bend to the right. As the road bends back left keep straight ahead onto a smaller road which then curves right to pass in front of the power station building. Immediately after the fish hatchery on the left look out for a blue marker post at the bottom of a small track heading uphill to the right. Turn up this and at the first bend turn left onto a small path. Ignore the steps down to the left, following the path as it climbs up to the main road.

Turn left along the road to pass Foyers Lodge; just beyond this take the path to the left (blue marker post and sign for Inverfarigaig). Climb a stile and follow the path until it emerges onto a tarred track. Turn right uphill and pass an electricity substation, taking the marked path on the left immediately beyond. This has some lovely glimpses of Loch Ness through the trees, eventually reaching a house. Follow the lane past more houses and a pier; from here follow the surfaced lane up to the main road. Turn left for a short distance and then turn right onto the Errogie road to return to the car park.

isolated aspect and in order to perform ceremonial magic there. The house was later owned by Led Zeppelin guitarist Jimmy Page, a Crowley enthusiast.

Eventually a forest track is reached; turn right to follow this downhill. The track bends left and passes the entrance of an old tunnel on the left. Keep straight on to pass the primary school and emerge onto the road opposite the church. Turn left to reach the main road; keep left here for a short section of road walking to Upper Foyers where there is a shop and café.

An Ire Mhor and the Change House

Distance 2.25km **Time** 1 hour
Terrain waymarked paths; steep climb and
descent in forestry plantation
Map OS Explorer 416
Access no public transport to start

**This short circular walk follows the shore
of Loch Ness to visit the site of an old inn.
After crossing the line of General Wade's
military road, the route climbs through
forestry to give views across the loch.**

   The walk starts from a lay-by
overlooking Loch Ness, with Urquhart
Castle visible on the far side. Follow the
path (SP Change House Path) along the
waterside, passing a number of seats –
perfect for a picnic. Soon An Ire Mhor is
reached, once the site of the tiny Change
House. Now reduced to a pile of stones,
this was once an inn where travellers

would have changed horses and rested up
for the night. The inn stood on the
military road running between Fort
Augustus and Inverness; folklore has it
that around the time of the Battle of
Culloden a government paymaster
carrying gold to the garrison at Fort
George to pay the soldiers' wages was
robbed and murdered here. The attackers
were never caught. Samuel Johnson and
James Boswell later stayed here in 1773
during their tour of the Highlands; they
were thoroughly unimpressed with the
accommodation and refreshment on
offer, describing it as 'a wretched hovel, of
earth only . . . and for a window had a hole
which was stopped with a piece of turf.'

   Head up to the road and then cross
carefully to take the path on the far side,
climbing through the forest plantations.

◀ The banks of Loch Ness from An Ire Mhor

The road undulates along much of the length of Loch Ness on its south side; it provides the course for the annual Loch Ness marathon. Many runners opt to dress as Nessie or in kilts as they run the 26.2-mile course, often raising money for Highland charities.

The path crosses a small bridge and then a clearing before reaching a bench with a good view across to Urquhuart Castle. Stay on the main track, ignoring a path to the right which heads up to the Fair Haired Lad's Pass – the top of the pass could be reached as an optional detour – a steep climb but with superb views from the top. The Pass is part of the newly created South Loch Ness Trail, a 45km walking route starting from Loch Tarff a few miles from Fort Augustus and finishing in Inverness.

Back on the main route, continue on the track before taking a sharp left onto a waymarked route leading downhill. At a bend look out for a path (marked) on the left and follow this down through the trees. When it levels off the route bears left alongside the plantation before emerging at the road near the ruins of a stone building and wall. Cross the road with care to return to the car park and picnic site.

Dores and Aldourie

Distance **6.5km** Time **2 hours**
Terrain **woodland paths and tracks;
sometimes muddy** Map **OS Explorer 416**
Access **bus (16) from Inverness to Dores**

**See if you have better luck than the Nessie
hunter on this fine circular walk along the
shores of Loch Ness and through the
woodland home of red squirrels.**

The walk starts through the car park
next to the Dores Inn (there is also a
parking bay on the main road in the
village opposite the telephone box). Take
the woodland path which runs behind
veteran Nessie hunter Steve Feltham's
caravan. Steve has been searching for the

monster since 1990, using a variety of
methods including trawling the 23-mile
loch with sonar equipped boats, and is
one of the most knowledgeable
Nessie enthusiasts. The path soon
reaches a children's play area. From here,
carry on along the back of the stony
beach with good views up Loch Ness, the
skyline dominated by the peak of Meall
Fuar-mhonaidh.

A gate leads into the trees; stay on the
wider, lower path at a fork and follow this
around the headland through the
pleasant woodland. Eventually, another
gate leads to the mooring at Aldourie
jetty and an old boatshed on the right

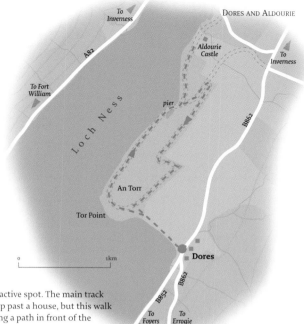

To Inverness

Aldourie Castle

To Inverness

A82

To Fort William

Loch Ness

pier

B862

An Torr

Tor Point

0   1km

Dores

B862

B852

To Foyers   To Errogie

– a very attractive spot. The main track continues up past a house, but this walk detours along a path in front of the house to get a view of impressive Aldourie Castle. At first the path is narrow and hemmed in by rhododendrons, but then it widens before reaching a gateway with a view of the 16th-century stone tower. The castle has been extended over the years, its last major rebuilding taking place in Victorian times. It is privately owned, so please respect this by not venturing past the gateposts, instead retracing the route back to the house near the jetty.

This time, turn left to head up the track, passing the house and eventually reaching a dilapidated wooden shack near the edge of the woodland. Turn right here onto a forest track, winding through the woods with the open fields always nearby on the left. At a T-junction with denser trees ahead, bear left. The path soon widens, passing mature beech trees, with views towards the Deer Pond on the left. As the woodland turns once again to pine, take a steep, rough path on the left to descend to the outward route near the gate at the entrance to the woods. Go through this and back along the shore path to return to the Dores Inn.

The Three Lochs round

Distance 12.5km **Time** 3 hours 30
Terrain wood and farmland paths and
tracks, sometimes boggy; quiet minor road
Map OS Explorer 416
Access no public transport to start

**Discover three peaceful lochs on the south
side of Loch Ness, all with their own
distinct character and a world away from
their big brother.**

Tucked away between the B862 from
Dores and the B851 at Farr, Loch
Duntelchaig and its surroundings are
little visited. Perseverance in reaching it is
rewarded with a wonderfully peaceful area
of lochs and rough moorland interspersed
by farmland and the odd settlement – it
could not feel further from the busy
honeypots along the north side of Loch
Ness and Inverness, only a few miles away
as the crow flies.

There is lay-by parking near to the
outlet just beyond the eastern end of
Loch Duntelchaig on the minor road
between Preas Dubh and Dunlichity. Start
the walk here by walking west towards
Loch Duntelchaig, soon passing the
popular fishing spot at Preas Dubh.
Follow the road as it heads uphill away
from the water and just before the crown
of the hill turn right through Easterton
Farm gate, signed for Bunachton. Follow
the track until just before a house, then
turn left on a footpath alongside it,
passing through two gates before the
path curves right through woodland.
The path can be waterlogged at times,
though a detour to the left should help
keep your feet dry. Soon the path climbs
and runs through forestry, passing some
ruined crofts before reaching a gate at a
minor road.

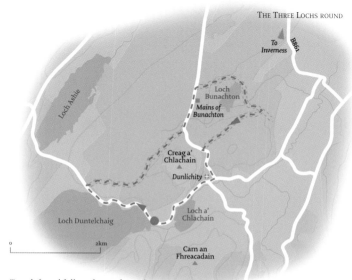

Turn left and follow the road, passing the Mains of Bunachton after which Loch Bunachton can be seen on the right. Halfway between here and the next plantation turn right through a gate onto a farm track heading diagonally towards the bottom corner of the forestry. A two-strand electric fence is sometimes in place across the track; this can be opened using the plastic handles but ensure you leave it as you found it. After another gate the track reaches the shore of Loch Bunachton, popular with grebes and other birds as well as fishermen.

Stay on the forestry track for another 1km before turning right at a clear junction. Remain on this track, ignoring a turn to the left, to eventually emerge on a minor road. Turn left to follow this

steeply downhill, then right at a T-junction to pass Dunlichity Church. The graveyard here is worth exploring; although the present day church dates from 1758 there has been a chapel on this site for much longer. Local folklore claims that soldiers from the Jacobite rebellion sharpened their swords on the walls on their way to the battle of Culloden – look carefully and you should be able to make out some grooves on a corner of the church wall.

Follow the road as it skirts the small but perfectly formed Loch a' Chlachain, another good spot for birdwatching. Eventually the quiet road winds its way back to the start point just short of Loch Duntelchaig.

◄ Tranquil Loch a' Chlachain

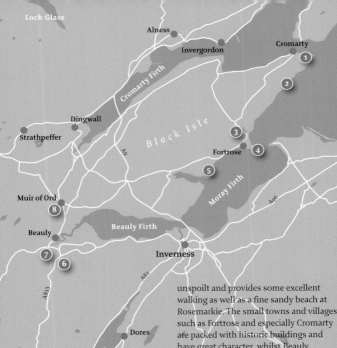

In spite of the name, the Black Isle is actually a peninsula to the north of Inverness, bounded by the Beauly Firth to the south and the Cromarty Firth to the north. Sheltered, largely low-lying, and known for its rich agricultural land, the Isle contrasts strongly with the other areas featured in this book, but is no less interesting for that. The coastline is unspoilt and provides some excellent walking as well as a fine sandy beach at Rosemarkie. The small towns and villages such as Fortrose and especially Cromarty are packed with historic buildings and have great character, whilst Beauly, usually thought to be just outside the Isle, has a celebrated deli and café as well as a ruined priory.

In addition to the walks here, the Black Isle has some fine country pubs, a distillery at Muir of Ord, and even its own beer – the Black Isle organic brewery producing some of Scotland's finest ales. With its renowned school of dolphins, quiet, unspoilt feel and easy access to many parts of the Highlands, the Isle has become a popular holiday destination in its own right.

Awaiting the dolphins at Chanonry Point ▶

The Black Isle and Beauly

Cromarty explorer

Distance 6.5km **Time** 2 hours
Terrain steep path to South Sutor, minor
road, then streets with pavements
Map OS Explorer 432 **Access** bus (26) from
Inverness and Fortrose to Cromarty;
summer car ferry links Cromarty to Nigg

Cromarty is one of the most fascinating
small towns in Scotland to explore. Climb
to the top of the South Sutor to appreciate
its strategic position at the mouth of the
Cromarty Firth before descending to
uncover the history of this Royal Burgh.

The narrow streets of Cromarty are
bursting with fascinating historical
buildings, each with a chapter to tell
about the prosperity or otherwise of this
shoreside settlement. Awarded the status
of a Royal Burgh in the 11th century,
Cromarty's early wealth was brought by
traders attracted by the harbour and
position at the mouth of the Cromarty
Firth, close to the fertile ground of the

Black Isle where hemp was a major
export. The oldest buildings date back 700
years and there are fine examples of
Georgian merchant houses and
fishermen's cottages as well as a good
smattering of Victorian properties.

There is a car park on the shore which is
signed as you come into the village; this
makes a good start to the walk. As you
face the sea from the car park turn right to
follow Shore Street along the coast,
passing an old salmon bothy and then the
ends of the rows of the fishermen's
cottages, built with their gables towards
the sea for protection. Opposite the
imposing red sandstone old brewery
building go left (SP South Sutor
Viewpoint) along Miller Road before
turning left onto a signed path just before
Clunes House. Once at the shore the path
follows it to the right; keep a keen eye out
for the dolphins that occasionally pass
through the straits here, sometimes

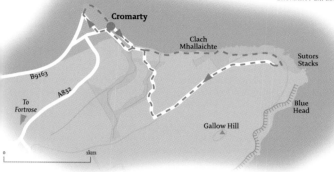

backed by the enormous bulks of oil rigs being towed to the maintenance yards at Invergordon.

Once it reaches the trees the path starts climbing across the headland. The cliffs flanking the entrance to the Cromarty Firth are known as the Sutors; opposite here, the North Sutor above Nigg makes a good, if often breezy, walk. When the path levels off briefly amongst mature beeches, dog leg to the left and then quickly turn right to continue climbing, with steps higher up. Pass the remains of St Mary's Well and then a well-preserved pill box from World War Two before the path eventually emerges from the woodland to reach the South Sutor viewpoint.

Turn right, following the road for 1.6km to a junction just short of Cromarty Mains Farm; turn right here to continue on the road downhill, passing The Stables arts venue and Cromarty House before returning to Miller Road. Back at the old Brewery turn left and then round the corner to the right to follow Church Street through the old heart of Cromarty. If time

allows, bob into the 700-year-old East Church on the left; no longer in use as a church, it was saved from dereliction after it appeared on the BBC's *Restoration* programme and has been beautifully restored. A short distance further on is a whitewashed thatched cottage, the birthplace of self-taught geologist, Hugh Miller; the cottage is now a fascinating museum. As Cromarty's most famous son, a statue of Miller stands on a high pillar overlooking the town – it can be reached by making a detour up The Paye just before the cottage. Otherwise continue along Church Street, passing the impressive clocktower of the Courthouse – now another museum – and the Victorian-built Hugh Miller Institute.

At the end of the road, turn left and then take a right along Bank Street to reach the harbour at its end. Bear right here to pass the creel and wildlife-watching boats. Just before the slipway for the tiny summer car ferry to Nigg, turn right onto a grassy path which leads back to the car park at the start.

◄ Cromarty from along the coast

Eathie Coast

Distance 4.5km **Time** 2 hours
Terrain clear but steep path to coast, then
pebbly shore; steep climb to return
Map OS Explorer 432 **Access** no public
transport to start

**A short but steep walk down to a hidden
section of the Black Isle coastline awash
with historical, geological and wildlife
interest. The route leads to an old salmon
bothy crammed with information on the
19th-century geologist, Hugh Miller.**

The walk starts from a small car park on
the back road off the A832 between
Rosemarkie and Cromarty. The car park is
just southwest of the buildings at Eathie
Mains and has an information board. The
walk down to the coast from here is said
to have been opened up by Hugh Miller,
the celebrated geologist who was born in
Cromarty in 1802. Take the track through
the gate and head towards the crest of the
hill. The Black Isle is renowned for its
fertile soil, with vegetables and barley
popular crops, and the rolling farmland is
spread out on the left. After passing a
small lochan the path starts to descend
through pinewoods towards the sea.

Although the ground is steep the path
is clear and descends in wide zigzags.
When it emerges onto the shore the
remains of an old salmon bothy can be
visited over to the right. This building was
used by salmon netters up until the mid-
1980s. Salmon netting involves the use of
'yairs' or large nets strung from stakes

driven into the seabed. These nets would then form a crescent shape to trap the fish at low tide. The bothy would have been the base for four men to fish here from February to August each year.

Walk past the front of the building; a short distance along the shore brings you to an older bothy which now houses information about salmon netting and Hugh Miller. Miller was born in Cromarty in 1802 and trained as a stonemason before combining his interests in nature and writing with evangelical Christianity. He made fossil discoveries while working in the local quarries which, combined with his self-taught geological knowledge, led him to theorise that the earth was in fact very old and that a great many species had lived on the planet at various times but had become extinct as new species emerged. Miller's life was short as he committed suicide aged 54, having published a large number of respected books but possibly having been suffering a form of psychotic depression – a large crowd attended his Edinburgh funeral and it is tempting to wonder how he might have developed his theories if he had lived longer.

The cliffs at Eathie are Devonian in origin and many Jurassic rocks are exposed on the wide shoreline at low tide. Although fossil hunters have denuded the area it is still possible to look for fossils among the rocks washed ashore or from the cliffs. You can walk in either direction along the coast, but take care to watch the incoming tide; at high tide most of the shoreline can be underwater. Heading north, you can continue to the Eathie Burn, whilst aiming south it is possible to hike all the way through to Rosemarkie at low tide. Otherwise when you have finished exploring the coast return by climbing the outward path back to the car park.

◄ Pebbly shoreline at Eathie

Fairy Glen, Rosemarkie

Distance 3km **Time** 1 hour
Terrain waymarked woodland path;
steps in places, can be muddy
Map OS Explorer 432 **Access** bus (26) from
Inverness and Cromarty to Rosemarkie

**A delightful wooded ravine with two
attractive waterfalls, the Fairy Glen is a
popular short walk from the interesting
village of Rosemarkie.**

There is a car park at the far end of
Rosemarkie as you leave the village on the
road to Cromarty. If walking from the
centre of the village, follow the main road
past the Plough Inn. The Fairy Glen is
now an RSPB reserve and there is an
information board in the car park. Take
the path upstream from the roadbridge.
The water from the glen was traditionally

used to support the two mainstays of the
Rosemarkie economy. In the 18th century,
flax was a popular local crop and the plant
would be soaked in a pond at the bottom
of the glen before it could be woven into
linen. In winter ice from the same pond,
together with the mill pond further up,
was used to fill a large icehouse which
preserved the salmon harvest en route
to market.

At a fork, branch right onto the smaller
path, keeping close to the burn. In spring,
the wood is carpeted with bluebells and
primroses; in all seasons, the native trees
provide a rich habitat for a variety of
birdlife. Cross a wooden footbridge and
continue up the far bank, passing the mill
pond which is at least 200 years old. Look
out for dippers bobbing on rocks in the

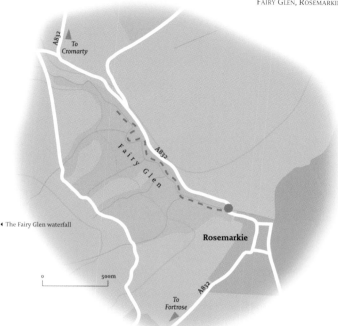

◀ The Fairy Glen waterfall

water nearby. The path soon crosses back over the burn at a second bridge to reach the first of the Fairy Glen's waterfalls. A well-dressing ceremony used to take place here – local children would traditionally decorate a pool near a spring with wildflowers to ensure the fairies kept the water supply sweet.

Climb the rough steps to the left of the cascade and cross the steep slope – a rope handrail provides security. The second of the waterfalls is just a short distance beyond. A footbridge leads

to a path climbing up to the main road, which can be used as an alternative return route though the road is narrow and relatively busy – it is much more enjoyable to retrace your steps down the glen.

If you have time, a visit to Groam House in Rosemarkie is recommended. This tiny museum holds an impressive collection of Pictish carved stones including a 3m-high carved red sandstone cross-slab known locally as 'the Soul of Rosemarkie'.

49

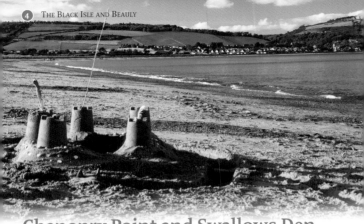

Chanonry Point and Swallows Den

Distance **8km** Time **3 hours 30**
Terrain **paths, beach, minor roads; very
steep (but avoidable) path up Swallows
Den** Map **OS Explorer 432** Access **bus (26)
from Inverness and Cromarty to Fortrose**

For those keen to see dolphins in their
natural environment Chanonry Point is
the best place on the British coastline. If
you catch these wonderful mammals
putting on a display you'll have to drag
yourself away to complete the rest of the
walk along a sandy beach to Rosemarkie
before taking a high route back to Fortrose
with great views.

At the heart of Fortrose are the ruins of
the 13th-century cathedral; there is
usually parking available near here. To
begin the walk return to the High Street
with the Anderson Inn on the corner and
turn left, passing a number of fine villas
before taking a sharp left along St

Andrews Walk. This leads down to the
harbour (SP Beach and sailing club);
continue on the road, passing a row of
pretty cottages. After climbing uphill turn
right at the junction by St Andrews
Church, passing Fortrose Academy.
Go through the picnic area on the right
and take a grassy path that continues into
Fortrose caravan park. Skirt around the
seaward side of the park to reach a three-
way signpost. Continue ahead (SP
Chanonry Point) through gorse bushes
and alongside the golf course before
reaching the sixth tee and the small
Chanonry Point car park.

Here a memorial marks the spot where
the Brahan Seer was burnt alive. The seer
is said to have foretold the building of the
Caledonian Canal, the collapse of the
Bonar Bridge, the Second World war and
the coming of the oil rigs at Nigg. He had
been employed by local landowners Lord

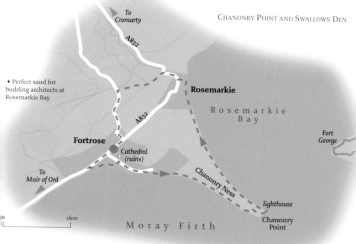

To Cromarty

A832

◀ Perfect sand for budding architects at Rosemarkie Bay

Rosemarkie

R o s e m a r k i e B a y

Fortrose

A832

Cathedral (ruins)

Fort George

To Muir of Ord

Chanonry Ness

lighthouse

Chanonry Point

M o r a y F i r t h

0   1km

and Lady Seaforth and pronounced during one of his visions that Lord Seaforth was having an affair in Paris. Lady Seaforth was outraged and ordered the seer to be placed in a spiked barrel which was filled with tar and set alight; a gruesome end.

Today, the lighthouse provides a more peaceful view across the Firth to Fort George. Head out along the pebbly shore to the Point itself, a mecca for dolphin enthusiasts. To maximise your chance of a sighting check the tide times with the Dolphin and Seal Centre (wdcs.org.uk) near the Kessock Bridge (open June to September) and try and time your visit to coincide with the bottlenose dolphins as they follow the fish in and out of the Firth with the tide. It's always a lottery, but the reward for perseverance is unforgettable – the dolphins often play in the water right by the Point and can sometimes be seen

catching and tossing fish and jumping only metres from the shore. The seasoned dolphin watchers who spend weeks at a time here can usually provide an update on the recent activity of the colony.

Continue around the peninsula on the beach or the shore path, passing Rosemarkie campsite and then picking up the seaside road. In the village follow the road inland to the Plough Inn and then turn right towards Cromarty. Watch out for a path on the left (SP Swallows Den) which climbs very steeply through the trees before following a sometimes overgrown path along the top of fields with great views back down over Fortrose and the Point. When the path emerges onto a lane turn left (SP Fortrose) and follow it down into the centre of the village to return to the start.

Ormond Castle

Distance **4.75km** Time **1 hour 30**
Terrain **easy tracks and minor roads; short, steep path to castle** Map **OS Explorer 432**
Access **bus (26) from Inverness and Cromarty to Avoch**

This easy circular walk from the old fishing village of Avoch visits the site of Ormond Castle; once an important medieval stronghold, it was later destroyed by Oliver Cromwell. Today the green mound offers excellent views back to the village and across the bay.

This walk starts at the southern end of Avoch (pronounced Och as in loch), a fishing village which grew up around the herring boom and had such a close-knit community that it even boasted its own dialect. Following the decline of the Kessock herring and white fish, fishing is no longer the mainstay of the village

economy, though the harbour still bustles with small boats, some offering trips to spot the local bottlenose dolphins. If you have time to explore the quaint streets of close-packed fishermen's cottages, seek out Lazy Corner for an artistic take on the modern bus shelter.

To reach the start follow the roads south through the village and along the shore of Avoch Bay where there is space to park at the end of the row of houses. Begin by walking up the minor road which climbs steeply away from the sea, ignoring the turning on the left to the industrial units. When the slope levels off turn left along a track (SP Ormond Castle). Just before Castleton Farm is reached go through a gate on the left, waymarked with a blue arrow, and follow the grassy path to pass just left of the grass-covered mound which is the site of

◀ Saltire flying at the remains of Ormond Castle overlooking Avoch

Ormond Castle, soon passing through a second gate.

Curve around the base of the mound before taking the small gate on the right to climb a narrow path up to the top. Once on the summit, the strategic position of this former fortress is clear, with good views over the Moray Firth and beyond. Although nothing remains of the castle today, the hill once boasted one of the largest strongholds in the Highlands. First built in the 12th-century, the castle served as part of William the Lion's defensive network and was the home of the De Moray family. In 1297 Andrew De Moray raised his standard here to rally his forces before marching to the support of William Wallace. Today the site is marked by a flagpole as well as a cairn and memorial plaque.

Return to the gate and then continue along the track towards the trees, ignoring the track to the right and staying on the main route. The forestry blocks any views down to the water apart from at one point with a seat. The track curves right and nears the edge of the trees; ignore a route branching right and continue ahead, soon passing between fields. Over to the left there

are views down to Munlochy Bay, an RSPB reserve popular with wading birds. If you are keen to see more, there is a viewing area off the A832 just east of Munlochy. When a surfaced road is reached turn right, then bear right again at the next junction with a minor road. This quiet lane passes through the rolling countryside before descending to Avoch Bay and the start.

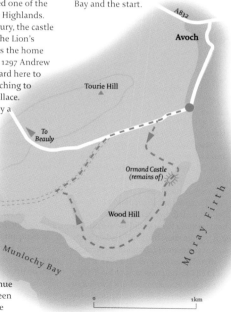

53

Phoineas Hill

Distance 4.75km **Time** 1 hour 30
Terrain waymarked forest paths and
tracks; gentle climb to hilltop
Map OS Explorer 431
Access no public transport to start

**Views over lower Strath Glass and
Beauly are the reward for this easy-going
climb to a hilltop mast in the forests
above Belladrum.**

To reach the start take the minor road
for Belladrum which branches off the
A833 at a lodge house 4km south of
Beauly. After passing a couple of houses
on the right there is limited parking at a
track entrance on the left with a
Belladrum Forest sign – take care to
ensure you do not obstruct the entrance.
From here the walk begins by heading up
the track, keeping an eye out for the red
squirrels that are plentiful here – they are

often heard and seen on the higher
branches of the pines. The track heads
gently uphill, curving to the right and
there are some good views over
Strathglass to be glimpsed through
the trees.

After 1.5km turn left at a junction of
forest tracks and continue climbing
before the route levels off for a time. After
a short distance turn left again at a
second junction, staying on the main
track and passing some rocky outcrops.
Soon turn left once more and follow the
track downhill to the next junction – this
time turn right. The route now climbs to
the summit of Phoineas Hill, crowned by
a small transmitter mast; despite its
diminutive height at only 180m it is a fine
viewpoint. The best outlook is from the
rocky summit on the far side of the mast.
Keep an eye out for red kites which have

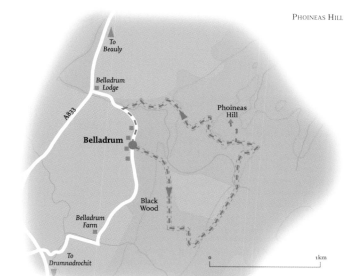

become a common sight here in recent years following their reintroduction; a rarer sighting would be the honey buzzard which breeds nearby.

To return head back down the track, turning right at the first junction. The route now winds downhill through the trees, eventually passing a picturesque estate cottage. Like much of the land in the Beauly area, the Belladrum Estate was once owned by the Lords of Lovat, chieftains of the Clan Fraser. They eventually sold it to the Stewarts, merchants in the 1820s. At this time the centrepiece of the estate was the large and elegant Belladrum House. In 1857 it was sold again to James Merry who enlarged

the house; his family owned the estate until it was sold off and broken up in the 1970s. By then Belladrum House had been demolished, having fallen into disrepair after the Second World War. Neighbouring Phoineas House was purchased by a descendant of James Merry who set about re-establishing much of the estate. The estate now hosts the annual Belladrum Tartan Heart music festival, the largest in northern Scotland, bringing together an eclectic mix of traditional, celtic, folk and modern music in a family-friendly atmosphere.

At the cottage turn left to follow a track back to the minor road, then left again to return to the start.

◀ Looking over Strath Glass from Phoineas Hill

River Beauly and Lovat Bridge

Distance 8km **Time** 2 hours 30
Terrain level paths, tracks and minor
roads; some navigation needed
Map OS Explorer 431
Access no public transport to start

**Watch for leaping salmon and the
fishermen trying to catch them as you
follow the graceful curve of the River
Beauly downstream. The return leg
crosses pleasant farmland bursting with
wild flowers.**

The walk starts at Black Bridge which
spans the River Beauly near Kilmorack; to
reach it from Inverness or Beauly, take the
A831 Cannich road from the A862 and
after 2km turn left signed for Kiltarlity.
There is a small parking area on the south
side of the bridge. To begin the walk cross
back over the bridge, noting the hydro-
power station seen upstream. On the far
side turn right and after a gate go up the
track into the trees. Ignore another track
leading down to the river on the right.
After 200m the track bends left; continue

on the smaller path ahead. At a small
clearing in the trees keep to the main path
on the right (the left-hand path is the
return route). As you head through the
trees there are glimpses of the river. The
path curves left to emerge in a grassy area
dotted with gorse bushes. At a fork bear
right to cross open land on a vague grassy
track. When the main Cruives Lodge track
is reached turn left, passing a weir on the
river and walking behind a red sandstone
house. Cross the road, continuing east on
a track that soon returns to the river.
A number of statuesque oaks line
the banks here; this is a popular spot
with anglers.

Stay on the main track, ignoring the
grassy branch that leads to the riverside.
The turrets of Beaufort Castle come into
view across the water. There has been a
castle here since the 12th century; for
many centuries it was the traditional clan
seat of the Frasers of Lovat. In 1303 the

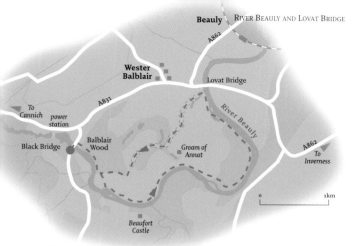

Beauly

A862

Wester Balblair

Lovat Bridge

A831

River Beauly

To Cannich

power station

Black Bridge

Balblair Wood

Groam of Annat

A862 To Inverness

0   1km

Beaufort Castle

original castle was besieged by the English during the first War of Scottish Independence. Centuries later, decades of sporadic fighting with the Macdonalds of Clanranald culminated in the 'Battle of the Shirts' – fought in 1544 and so named because the warm weather meant the 1000 men, of whom it is said only 12 survived, fought in their shirts. Later the Frasers supported Bonnie Prince Charlie at the battle of Culloden, providing over 400 men for the front line. Following the defeat the Fraser lands were forfeited to the Crown and the castle was destroyed. Later the fortunes of the clan improved and the present-day castle was built in the 1870s; it now belongs to Ann Gloag, co-founder of the Stagecoach bus company.

Just before the track bends right to reach the river, look out for a path heading straight on through the gorse on the left. This soon becomes clearer and joins the riverbank, passing in front of a white house and over a small bridge to join a track. Continue through a gate and into the woods, remaining on the main track as it meanders away from the river, ignoring a turn to the right. It soon returns once again to the riverside to pass a fishing hut. Continue to a gate and past some houses with a view of Lovat Bridge ahead. At a stand of fir trees and a stable building turn left along a track. This passes a new house to reach a minor road; turn left along the road and continue for approximately 2km, ignoring any side tracks. After passing a farm look out for a telegraph pole with a track off to the right and take this often muddy route which skirts the edge of a wood on a clearer path. Keep the trees on your right as you pass the remains of a building to rejoin the outward route. Turn right along the riverside path and track to return to Black Bridge.

◀ *Along the banks of the wide River Beauly*

Ord Hill

**Distance 4km Time 2 hours
Terrain waymarked forestry tracks and
paths; steep uphill section and short,
boggy section Map OS Explorer 431
Access no public transport to start**

This short hill walk climbs through
woods and crosses heather moorland
to reach the summit of Cnoc Croit na
Maoile – a fine viewpoint for the
Cromarty and Beauly Firths with the
Black Isle between.

The walk starts a short distance
southwest of Muir of Ord; to reach it
follow one of the the minor roads leading
towards Corry of Ardnagrask from the
A862, and then follow the sign for Upper
Aultvaich. There is limited space to park

where the road bends sharply to the left
and a forestry track leads straight ahead.
There is also space for one car near the
gateway a wee bit back down the road;
either way, take care not to block any
gates or other access.

Start the walk by heading through the
gate (SP Ord Hill) and along the forestry
track into Corry Wood, a mix of Scots
pine, birch and hazel. As the track
narrows, the yellow of the broom and
gorse provides a colourful display for
much of the year. Gradually the views
open up behind with the Kessock Bridge
near Inverness visible in the distance
beyond the Beauly Firth.

Turn sharp left at a signed junction to
climb more steeply through the trees; this

section can be very wet underfoot at times. Soon the path emerges onto heather moorland; cast a glance skyward for circling birds of prey or skylarks. The gradient eases and when the edge of the wood on the right is reached bear sharp right (SP Ord Hill).

The final climb soon leads to the summit of Cnoc Croit na Maoile – or Ord Hill as it is commonly known. The seat built around the trig point makes a perfect spot handy for admiring the 360-degree view. Looking towards the coast, the waters of the Cromarty and Beauly Firths are split by the fertile Black Isle between. Looking west provides a view into the mountains above Glen Affric and Strathfarrar.

Continue on the path past the trig point, heading east downhill to soon join a wider path. Bear left onto this to soon rejoin the outward route. Retrace the outward climb with great views across the Beauly Firth for most of the return.

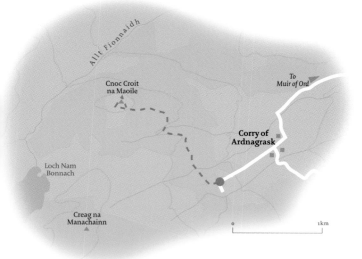

◀ Looking out to sea from Ord Hill

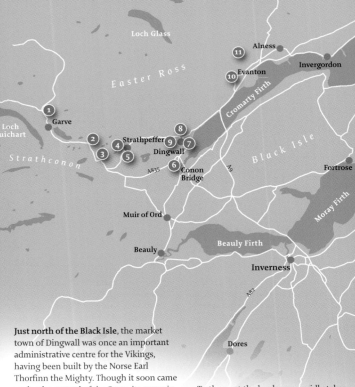

Just north of the Black Isle, the market town of Dingwall was once an important administrative centre for the Vikings, having been built by the Norse Earl Thorfinn the Mighty. Though it soon came under the control of the Scots, its name is a reminder of these origins, being Norse for the 'meeting place'. The town today retains a distinctive feel and is an excellent base for exploring the region. Neighbouring Strathpeffer is in stark contrast, its pump rooms and Pavilion being palpable reminders of its heyday as a Victorian spa resort.

To the west the landscape rapidly takes on a Highland character, passing through the great forests around Contin and past the foaming Rogie Falls to reach the small village of Garve and on to the mountains beyond. East of Dingwall the main roads north stick tightly to the coastline of the Cromarty Firth, overlooked by the great monument on Fyrish hill.

Autumn colours on the Black Water ▶

Dingwall, Strathpeffer and Easter Ross

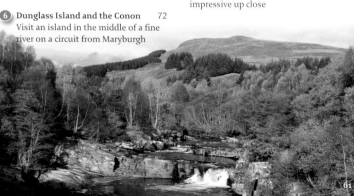

Silverbridge and Little Garve

Distance **3.5km** Time **1 hour 30**
Terrain **waymarked woodland paths**
Map **OS Explorer 437**
Access **no public transport to start**

Following the banks of the Black Water between two ancient stone bridges is a delight in any season. There is plenty of wildlife amongst the pines and some great picnic spots by the river.

The walk starts at Silverbridge 3km north of Garve, but you can also start from the parking area at Little Garve, or if feeling more energetic walk from the centre of Garve itself. The Silverbridge car park is on the north side of the road just before it crosses the Black Water. The car park has toilets and an information board; the walk starts by heading down a path near the entrance to cross the old stone bridge that gives the walk its name – it sits redundant to vehicular traffic following the construction of the modern crossing of the busy A835 Inverness to Ullapool road.

Whilst modern transport links are now taken for granted, in the aftermath of the 1715 Jacobite rebellion moving across the Highlands was a different matter. The massive road building project overseen by General Wade and continued by Major Caulfield was to transform the landscape, enabling troops to move around quickly to suppress any future rebellions. Both the bridges on this walk formed part of General Wade's route north and, although much of the actual road is gone, the beautiful stone bridges still stand as fine monuments. Silverbridge spans a boiling tumble of water and construction must have been quite a feat of engineering.

Once over the bridge turn right to pass under the modern road bridge and into woodland to reach a track near a couple of houses. Head to the right along the track for about 0.5km, keeping an eye out for a

◂ Wade Bridge over the Black Water

waymarked path to the right. This leads into the woods, with a fine view ahead over the river at one point. Eventually the path descends to the banks of the Black Water as it forces its way around and over rocky slabs, boulders and tranquil pools on its way towards the Beauly Firth. This area is great for wildlife – in spring and summer it teems with birdlife and woodland flowers, whilst late summer and autumn can produce some startling fungi; this is also a good time to watch for leaping salmon as they fight their way upstream. Look out also for roe deer flitting through the trees; pine martens and wildcat also live here though you'd be very lucky to see one.

Eventually a stile brings you out onto a track; turn right to head across the second of the old bridges. Though known as Wade Bridge, this was built by General Caulfield in 1762, and has a much more pronounced hump than the Silverbridge. The route here forms part of a much older drove route, on which cattle would have been driven to the big markets of the south at towns such as Crieff and Falkirk.

Little Garve was a traditional resting spot, where cattle would often be shod in preparation for the harder roads ahead.

Once over the bridge turn right into the woods; the Little Garve parking area is close by here. At an information board, bear right to join a wide path which runs alongside the river – here lined by some magnificent old Scots pines. After a beautiful meander upstream, the route heads back under the road bridge to emerge at Silverbridge and the start.

To Ullapool

Silverbridge

A835

Torr Breac

0   500m

To Achnasheen

A832

Gorstan

To Inverness

Little Garve

Wade Bridge

Black Water

Rogie Falls

Distance 1.5km **Time** 1 hour
Terrain **waymarked forest footpaths; rocky**
and steep in places Map **OS Explorer 437**
Access **no public transport to start**

Watch for leaping salmon at the
thundering Rogie Falls from the bridge
suspended over the river.

The Rogie Falls car park is well signed
from the A835 north of Inverness and just
west of Contin, and has toilets open in
the summer. Begin by following the
waymarked path (red and green) down
through the pines and silver birch trees.
When you reach a crossroads, turn left
(green waymarker) and follow the
narrower path which climbs for a short

while before winding downhill between
lichen-draped trees and boulders to reach
the Black Water. Here bear right to
shadow the river downstream. The Black
Water drains a vast catchment area, some
of which is diverted to power a hydro-
electric scheme.

The path soon reaches Rogie Falls where
a viewing area gives a close-up view of the
foaming water, although the falls are
much better seen from the metal
suspension bridge just below. To reach it,
ignore the red waymarked path and take
the path leading down to the river. The
bridge, which the local council advises
should take only five people at once,
spans high above the river and provides a

◄ Suspension bridge overlooking Rogie Falls

grandstand view. Between June and October keep your eyes peeled for salmon attempting to leap the falls. Their passage is eased by a fish ladder on the far side of the falls which was provided when the hydro scheme was built; this enables salmon to bypass the falls and access the higher reaches of the river when water levels are artificially low. The salmon still seem to prefer the challenge of the falls and it's an amazing sight to see the same fish persevering with numerous attempts before finally continuing its journey to the spawning grounds upstream.

Quieter sections of the river provide good spots to watch dippers on rocks in the water and a number of other birds. A path ascends on the

far side of the falls, climbing up to reach a forestry track that links with Garve and with the View Rock walk at Contin. However, to continue the short Rogie Falls circular, return back across the river and bear left following the red waymarked route. At a fork aim left to the Raven's Crag viewpoint which offers a great view of the suspension bridge backed by the falls. From here return to the last junction and turn left to climb a series of zigzags through the forest. This soon reaches the crossroads passed earlier; turn left here and the car park is a few steps further on.

To Lochluichart

A835

Black Water

Rogie Falls

Cnoc Dubh

0   500m

To Contin

View Rock, Contin

Distance 4.5km **Time** 1 hour 30
Terrain easy going, waymarked forest
tracks and paths **Map** OS Explorer 437
Access bus (27) from Dingwall and
Inverness to Contin

Torrachilty Forest extends for many miles
on the southern flanks of Ben Wyvis, with
patches of native ash and birches amongst
the mass of spruce and pines; in its most
remote corners the forest is thought to
harbour wildcat. This pleasant circuit
climbs through the section closest to
Contin to reach a viewpoint.

The whole area from Strathpeffer to
Garve has scores of forest tracks and
paths popular with both walkers and
cyclists. In recent years the forest has
hosted the annual Strathpuffer endurance
mountain bike event. Timed to coincide
with the short days and harsh weather of

the Scottish winter, this gruelling
challenge sees teams and individuals
compete to complete as many rounds of
the undulating 11km course of bog or
frozen ground as they can in 24 hours.

The route starts from the Forestry
Commission car park signed off the A835
just north of Contin. There are
information boards about the extensive
path network in the area as well as public
toilets (summer only). Torrachilty is very
much a working forest so tree harvesting
may be taking place on the route, in which
case follow any diversion signs. This route
is waymarked in green; start by following
the trail across the picnic area (SP Forest
Walk). Climb through birch woodland and
cross two forestry tracks, staying on the
green waymarked path.

At a third track aim right, crossing the
track to follow the sign for View Rock.

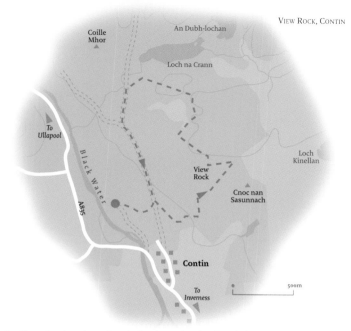

An Dubh-lochan

Coille
Mhor

Loch na Crann

To
Ullapool

Black Water

A835

View
Rock

Loch
Kinellan

Cnoc nan
Sasunnach

Contin

To
Inverness

0   500m

Continue ahead on the path and when it dips to another track, cross this to continue on the path ahead. The route passes through an area of felled trees before it re-crosses the track and heads uphill. The cleared section of forest provides good views over the surrounding countryside before the path plunges back into the dark forest, passing a seat near the remains of a stone wall.

When you reach a fork, a short detour to the left leads to View Rock, a panoramic viewpoint for Loch Achilty and Ross-shire beyond, though it is gradually becoming obscured by the trees. This is a good spot for a break and, if quiet, you may well see roe deer wandering amongst the clearings. From here, return to the path and continue until you reach a wide track; go left and head gently downhill. Look out for the green waymarker where the route bears left onto a narrower path. At the next junction turn left (SP Contin), soon emerging onto a forestry track at a large boulder.

Turn left along the track (SP Contin), eventually meeting the green marked path to the right used earlier in the walk. Bear right down the path, crossing the two tracks, before returning to the car park.

◀ Loch Achilty glimpsed through the trees of Torrachilty Forest

Loch Kinellan and Ord Wood

Distance **6km** Time **2 hours 30**
Terrain **tracks and paths; rough in places**
Map **OS Explorer 437** Access **bus (27) from
Dingwall and Inverness to Strathpeffer**

**Head north from the Victorian spa village
of Strathpeffer, climbing through the
woods and visiting Loch Kinellan with its
ancient crannog.**

This walk starts from the centre of
Strathpeffer which can easily absorb half a
day pottering around. Following the
discovery of a sulphurous spring in the
1800s and amid miraculous claims for the
healing powers of the water, Strathpeffer
soon developed to become a popular
Victorian spa. The pump room in the
centre of the village – which now serves
as the tourist information centre – was
built in 1819 and was closely followed by a
hospital and later the Pavilion. The arrival
of the railway in 1885 really put

Strathpeffer on the map and many of the
grand hotels and elegant villas date from
around this time. The Spa Pavilion has
recently been restored and now hosts a
wide range of events including
exhibitions and concerts; you can also
sample the waters here.

Begin the walk by heading up Golf
Course Road opposite the Pavilion,
passing the Wee Swally tea room and a
fine turreted house. Continue uphill and
turn left at a crossroads beyond the
church, marked with the deer logo of the
local footpath network. At another fork
take the higher road on the right, passing
some attractive cottages. Keep an eye out
for a path on the right heading into Ord
Wood. Follow this past gravestones,
heading through the gate into the trees
before turning right at the next junction.
The path skirts the lower edge of the
woods, providing views over Strathpeffer,

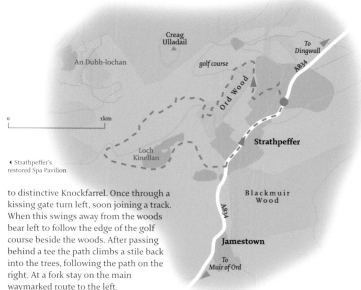

Creag
Ulladail

An Dubh-lochan

golf course

To
Dingwall

A834

Ord Wood

0   1km

Loch
Kinellan

Strathpeffer

◀ Strathpeffer's
restored Spa Pavilion

Blackmuir
Wood

A834

Jamestown

To
Muir of Ord

to distinctive Knockfarrel. Once through a
kissing gate turn left, soon joining a track.
When this swings away from the woods
bear left to follow the edge of the golf
course beside the woods. After passing
behind a tee the path climbs a stile back
into the trees, following the path on the
right. At a fork stay on the main
waymarked route to the left.

When you reach the footpath sign it is
possible to shortcut back to Strathpeffer;
however, the complete walk turns right
(SP Kinellan) and follows the curving path
which eventually leaves the woods at a
stile. Follow the path over now open
countryside, crossing a footbridge and
then bearing left to climb a high stile.
Turn right to follow the track (SP Kinellan
Viewpoint and Contin). After 0.5km turn
onto a clear path on the left and at a fork
branch left (waymarker). Pass a seat and
keep left at the next two forks to reach a
track, then turn right (SP Contin and
Garve). Bear left again at the next junction
and go through a gate to pass the far end

of Loch Kinellan. In the late 15th century
the banks of this loch bore witness to a
bloody clan battle when the local
Mackenzies defeated a large invading
force of Macdonalds. The wooded island
has grown up on the remains of a
crannog, an artificial island built to
provide a living place safe from wolves or
raiding humans in iron-age times. It was
from here that the Mackenzie chief set out
to defend his people. When you reach the
road turn right, following it until it
emerges on the A834 opposite the former
Youth Hostel (now converted to private
flats). Turn left along the pavement back
into the centre of Strathpeffer.

69

Knockfarrel from Strathpeffer

Distance 7km **Time** 2 hours
Terrain clear paths, muddy in places;
extremely steep (but avoidable) descent
Map OS Explorer 437 **Access** bus (27) from
Dingwall and Inverness to Strathpeffer

Climb through forests to visit a geological maze en route to the ancient fort atop the distinctive hill of Knockfarrel. A ridge walk then leads on to Cnoc Mor before a steep descent back to Strathpeffer.

This walk starts from the Blackmuir Wood Forestry car park at the west end of Strathpeffer; on the right if approaching the village on the A834 from Contin. Begin by taking the waymarked path from the car park, soon passing a lochan and reaching a forestry track. Turn right along this to a cluster of log cabins, then left through a gate, continuing on the track with an area of felled trees on the left.

Soon take a path on the left (SP Ring Path) which winds through densely-planted spruces and passes a bench.

Eventually another path joins from the left and the route nears the edge of the trees, allowing views over Strathpeffer village. Cross a track and at a fork branch left to find the stone maze. The maze – not one in which anyone would get lost – is actually a modern arrangement of 81 stones representing the different rocks found around Scotland. It is based on the design of prehistoric labyrinths where the stones were aligned with the solstices and played an important part in pagan festivals. Beyond the maze follow the waymarked path, bearing left onto a wider path and continuing to reach a larger track. Go left along this, eventually leaving the forest at a stile. Continue along the track, ignoring the path which branches steeply uphill.

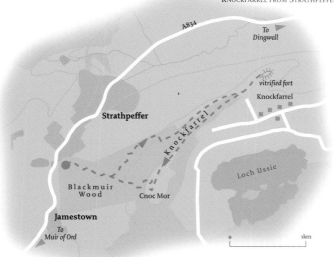

The track climbs gently to gain the ridge at the low point between Knockfarrel and the higher Cnoc Mor ridge. Once on the ridge bear left to reach the wide, grassy summit of Knockfarrel, site of an iron-age fort whose vitrified walls are still visible in places. There are a number of these forts in the northeast of Scotland as well as Ireland and mainland Europe, but none have been discovered in England or Wales.

After enjoying the wide-ranging views over the Beauly Firth and beyond, retrace your steps to the low point and then continue west along the ridge. The path passes a seat and a small but striking modern sculpture of three embracing figures. Continue ahead at the next dip on the ridge unless you want to avoid the steep final descent (in which case it is possible to turn right to go down, then left at a track to return to the start). If pressing ahead to Cnoc Mor, climb the stile and keep the forest fence on your right. The route follows the undulating heather ridge, with good views to Loch Ussie in places, until the final climb to the summit of Cnoc Mor and its trig point.

From here cross the stile to head into the forest, keeping right each time the path forks. The path traverses steep slopes before turning left just before a stile to descend sharply. Stay on the main path, eventually reaching a wider one; turn right here then left at a track to return to the start.

◀ Overlooking Dingwall and the Beauly Firth from Knockfarrel

Dunglass Island and the Conon

Distance 12km **Time** 3 hours 30
Terrain riverside and farm paths, quiet
track; can be muddy **Map** OS Explorer 432
Access bus (25) from Dingwall and
Inverness to Maryburgh

**Often overlooked by visitors, this
circuit explores the banks of the River
Conon before returning through the
woods to Maryburgh.**

Maryburgh is a small village which grew
up to house crofters from the Brahan
estate and elsewhere who were displaced
from higher up Strathconon by the
Highland Clearances in the 1800s.
Its position on the banks of the River
Conon made it an ideal site for a number
of mills including ones for corn, meal,
lint and snuff.

There is limited parking on the bridge
just east of the war memorial at the north
end of Maryburgh. From here head back
along the main street staying on the
pavement when the road leaves to cross
the railway. Continue into Seaforth Place

and about half-way up the hill look out
for some steps on the left which lead to
Muirdean Road. Bear left at the junction
and go straight ahead on Muirdean Road
when the main road bends right. At the
end of the road take the grassy path
between the houses and the railway.

Don't cross the footbridge over the
railway; instead remain on the path which
soon runs parallel to Stuarthill Drive and
eventually reaches a stile. Ignore the level
crossing to stay on the clear path between
the trees on the left and the field on the
right. The small paths which head down
to the river are mainly used by fishermen
and are often flooded.

After about 1km the bridge to Dunglass
island – a large island of arable and
woodland set in a split in the River Conon –
is reached. Cross the bridge and turn left to
follow the path around the field edge.
The natural defences of the river led to the
island being the site of an iron-age fort.

Before the trees at the north end of the
island are reached follow the path to cut

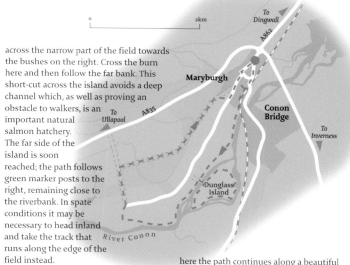

across the narrow part of the field towards the bushes on the right. Cross the burn here and then follow the far bank. This short-cut across the island avoids a deep channel which, as well as proving an obstacle to walkers, is an important natural salmon hatchery. The far side of the island is soon reached; the path follows green marker posts to the right, remaining close to the riverbank. In spate conditions it may be necessary to head inland and take the track that runs along the edge of the field instead.

After a bench overlooking a weir, continue along the riverside to pass a hut overlooking a more tranquil pool. Soon cross a bridge over the water channel (if this is flooded head to the right to reach the track and turn left along it to catch up with the route further on). Follow the path after the bridge to a fishing hut and weir. In dry weather it is possible to shorten the walk here by crossing the weir to resume the walk up the Conon, though the rocks can be very slippery. Otherwise, follow the track which soon leads back to the bridge to leave the island.

Cross and turn left to continue along the field edge near to the river, eventually passing the other side of the weir. From here the path continues along a beautiful stretch of riverside before heading uphill to the right of a wood. At a stile turn right to climb along an earth bank to reach a track. At the track bear left along the road towards Brahan House. The road leads into woodland and reaches a crossroads with tracks – turn right here, passing a cottage along a wide avenue of trees. There are distant views out to the Cromarty Firth. Keep on the track as it re-enters the wood, ignoring the path to the left. After a metal gate keep right at a fork to descend through the trees towards houses on the edge of Maryburgh. When the path emerges onto a road turn left. At the next T-junction turn left again to return to the main road at the war memorial.

◀ The banks of the River Conon

73

Macdonald Monument

Distance **6km** Time **2 hours**
Terrain **waymarked footpath, track, road
with pavement** Map **OS Explorer 432**
Access **buses (25, 27) and trains from
Inverness to Dingwall**

**Dingwall enjoys a fine setting near the
head of the Cromarty Firth; this enjoyable
walk heads down to the former harbour
area before climbing inland to visit the
Macdonald Monument above the town.**

Dingwall – famed for the quality of its
haggis – is a good place to while away a
morning or afternoon moseying around
the shops and hostelries. Its position by
the Cromarty Firth gave rise to its
importance as a settlement in Norse
times, and despite today being dwarfed by
nearby Inverness, Dingwall has a lot to
commend it, especially its easy access
to the pleasant countryside and coast.

The walk begins from the town
centre; there is a large car park south
of the High Street which is signed
from the A862. The start of this walk

is at the museum which is housed in the
Town Hall on the High Street, easily
recognised by its distinctive clocktower.
Follow the High Street to the right before
taking a left along Tulloch Street, passing
a supermarket and furniture shop. Look
out for a path off to the right alongside
the canal (SP Ferry picnic site). Head along
this; the canal was dug in 1817 with the
aim of re-establishing Dingwall as a port
with a large harbour on the Cromarty
Firth. Like many civic engineering projects
in the Highlands it was designed by the
seemingly workaholic Thomas Telford.
However, the builders ignored Telford's
advice not to let the River Peffery flow
into the canal and as a result the canal
regularly silted up before being
abandoned in 1840.

Cross the railway line with
care, following the path
alongside the caravan park
towards the open water or
mudflats of the Cromarty Firth.
Ignore the footbridge and stay

on the right side of the canal, soon reaching the picnic area. Take the path around the edge of the small park which is a good spot to watch for birds, in particular overwintering greylag geese, wigeon and goldeneye. The sculpture here is a model of the much larger Fyrish Monument (see page 82) which dominates the view when heading north from Dingwall.

At a junction of paths keep left and at the entrance driveway to the picnic site turn left to leave it. At the crossroads a left turn brings you back to the estuary where the route continues over a footbridge. Keep on the coastal path (SP Round Dingwall walk) passing an old bothy at Pitglassie before heading inland on a track which crosses the railway and then passes under the main road. After the tunnel bear right along the road, then turn left towards Pitglassie, heading towards a farm. Just before the first farm building turn right and climb more steeply before the road levels off with views of the Macdonald Monument over to the right. The tower was built between 1904-07 to commemorate Sir Hector 'Fighting Mac' Macdonald, a local crofter's son who rose through the ranks of the 92nd Gordon Highlanders, eventually taking command

of the army in Ceylon. However, having also made enemies, rumours around his sexuality made life unbearable for Macdonald who committed suicide in a Parisian hotel room. His supporters erected this monument in his memory and it is visible from most of Dingwall.

After a wood on the right go through a gate and turn sharp right onto a minor road which leads towards the cemetery and heads steeply downhill. At the fork you can visit the Monument by a short detour before returning down the road to reach the main A862. Turn left here before crossing with care to return to the car park and the high street beyond.

◀ The Macdonald Monument above Dingwall

Tulloch Castle ramble

Distance 5.5km **Time** 2 hours
Terrain waymarked paths, track and road
with pavement **Map** OS Explorer 432
Access buses (25, 27) and trains from
Inverness to Dingwall

**Explore the pleasant hill slopes on the
northern side of Dingwall on this
straightforward circuit, looping past
Tulloch Castle, now a hotel. The walk
should leave plenty of time to nose about
the independent shops and cafés of
Dingwall's High Street.**

Dingwall is a town with a long history;
once perhaps the Viking capital of
Scotland, it has managed to keep a good
range of shops and eateries despite its
close proximity to Inverness. If driving,
there is a large car park just south of the
High Street, signed from the A862. To
reach the starting point head past the
public toilets, following a narrow walkway
before turning right on the High Street to
reach the clock-towered Town Hall and
Museum. From here continue east along
the street until Tulloch Street where you
turn left, eventually passing the old canal
and railway.

At the A862 turn right and cross the
road, continuing on the far side until the
fine villas are left behind and a path heads
left (SP Craig Wood). Follow this path as it
climbs through the trees and then turn
left at a signed junction. Climb uphill
along a line of beech trees beside a fence
and field. As height is gained there are
good views over Dingwall and the
Cromarty Firth. At a minor road go
straight across to head up the lane
opposite, soon bearing right onto a

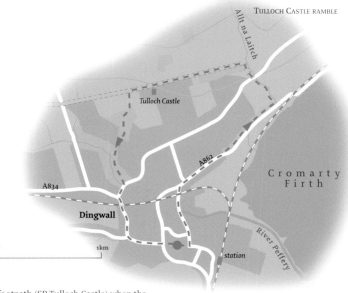

Allt na Laitch

Tulloch Castle

A862

A834

Dingwall

1km

C r o m a r t y
F i r t h

River Peffery

station

footpath (SP Tulloch Castle) when the road curves left. Keep straight ahead; after a stile the path crosses open ground, with the wall which once enclosed Tulloch Castle's walled garden on the left. After farm buildings the rear entrance of Tulloch Castle is reached – you can detour left here for a closer look.

Originally built in the 1540s as a tower house, Tulloch Castle has been extended many times over the centuries. The castle became the home of Clan Davidson following its purchase by Henry Davidson, a London sugar merchant in the 1760s, and it remained in the Davidson family until the Tulloch lands were gifted to the local council. The castle was then used as a boarding hostel for pupils from

remote areas to attend Dingwall Academy. Later the property came into private ownership and it is now run as a hotel.

Return to the track behind the castle and continue to the left. At the next junction bear left (SP Maggie's Path) and cross open ground with good views of Knockfarrel Hill over to the right. The grassy path soon heads into the trees.

Keep right at a fork and then keep left at the next junction. At a crossroads continue ahead to eventually emerge onto a road. Aim left here and soon the main Dingwall to Strathpeffer road is reached. Turn left to follow the road back to the traffic lights near the centre of Dingwall. Cross at the lights to return to the High Street.

◀ Tulloch Castle Hotel

77

Knockfarrel from Dingwall

Distance 12.5km **Time** 3 hours 30
Terrain **waymarked paths, track and road**
with pavement; one steep climb
Map **OS Explorer 432 Access** **buses (25, 27)**
and trains from Inverness to Dingwall

Climb up through farmland to explore
the Iron-Age fort of Knockfarrel, a
fantastic viewpoint overlooking Dingwall
and the Cromarty Firth.

Dingwall is easily reached by bus or
train from Inverness and has a large free
car park just south of the High Street,
signed from the A862. The walk starts
only a few steps away at the Museum and
clock-towered Town Hall on the High
Street. To begin, head west along the
High Street, passing the council
buildings. At the traffic lights go
straight across, following the

A834 and passing the police headquarters.
When the main road bends left continue
straight ahead up Blackwells Street
towards Knockbain. This road soon
narrows to a quiet lane and starts to climb
steadily. At a fork branch left onto
Knockbain Road; Tulloch Castle can be
seen in the distance over on the right.

At the entrance to Knockbain House
keep left and then straight ahead at the
next fork to avoid Knockbain Farmhouse.
The track now climbs through more open
farmland, passing a barn and a section of
forestry. The views looking back out over
the Cromarty Firth, often dotted with oil
rigs lined up for repair at Invergordon,
open up as height is gained.

After a kissing gate the distinctive
outline of Knockfarrel can be seen
ahead. Formed from the remains of

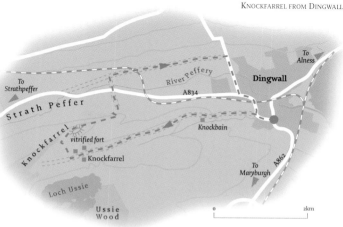

molten lava from an ancient volcano, erosion over time has left the harder rock exposed. Once the track levels off, keep straight ahead through a gate (SP Strathpeffer) to eventually meet the road. Pass a phonebox, post office and then two more houses, before turning right along a road leading to a single house. Beyond this take a left-hand fork to follow the track up to a parking area on the lowest point of the ridge of Knockfarrel hill.

Bear right here to climb up to the summit of the fort. The method of construction of this 3000-year old stronghold continues to mystify archaeologists. The stones of the fort have been vitrified – heated to such a high temperature that they fused together, though how such high temperatures were achieved is a matter of speculation. The shape of the former ramparts can still be made out, though they are better seen

from the air. At the far end of the fort follow a narrow path down the nose of the hill, enjoying the expansive views in all directions.

Climb a stile and look out for a sign for Fodderty, taking the path on the left. This heads downhill to another stile. Cross this and turn left to cross the old railway line to reach the main road. Carefully cross and take the lane opposite, soon turning right at the T-junction. The track passes through farmland, crosses the railway at a level crossing and narrows after Brae Farm Cottages. Go through two sets of kissing gates and pass the sheds of Docharty Farm before taking the signed route between cottages to avoid passing through the farmyard. Once back on the original lane a minor road is soon reached. Turn right here, right at the next junction, and finally left at the main road to return to the centre of Dingwall.

◂ Dingwall Town Hall

Black Rock Gorge

Distance 4km **Time** 1 hour 30
Terrain woodland paths and tracks, can
be very muddy, minor road; care needed
near gorge **Map** OS Explorer 432
Access bus (25) from Dingwall, Inverness
and Tain to Evanton

**This short ramble through the
woods reveals the Black Rock Gorge, a
seemingly bottomless chasm through
which Harry Potter fled his pursuers in
the film *The Goblet of Fire.***

If driving, park in the main car park in
the centre of Evanton, opposite the
Cornerstone bookshop and café. Cross the
road and take the side road off between
the Co-op and the Post Office, heading
towards the imposing chapel at the far
end. Before this is reached, turn right up
Camden Street, and at the end of this
street continue onto a track (SP Black
Rock Gorge) which curves left uphill. After

leaving the houses behind, the tree-lined
track reaches a junction; go straight ahead
though a gateway here. Fyrish Monument
can be seen on the horizon over the field
to the right.

Once in the wood a junction of tracks is
reached – bear slightly right here to follow
a track high above the River Glass; there is
a small sign for the gorge on a tree which
can be hard to spot. Keep straight on
when another track is joined and keep an
eye out for a path on the right after a very
short distance. This leads downhill, once
more marked with a very small sign.
At the bottom of the hill the first of two
bridges over the gorge is reached. Detour
to view the gorge from this first bridge
before returning to continue on the
path along the near side of the gorge to
reach a second footbridge, this one giving
a much more impressive view of this
dramatic chasm.

◀ Staring into the abyss – Black Rock Gorge

Black Rock Gorge is a box canyon formed by water eroding a softer band of rock and leaving a deep and twisting ravine with the surging water of the River Glass seen far below. The dark walls of the gorge are moss-covered, supporting ferns and even the odd tree growing horizontally in the damp atmosphere. With the eerie appearance of the gorge, it makes the perfect setting for supernatural tales. It's no surprise that this remote location was chosen for a scene in the 2004 film, *Harry Potter and the Goblet of Fire* – the single scene in which Harry was chased into the gorge took 10 days to shoot.

Cross the bridge and climb the path on the far side. This is often muddy; if required, a drier option is to retrace the outward route back to Evanton. To continue the circuit, the path levels as it bends right and widens to become a track along the edge of a field. Remain on the main track, ignoring any turnings, to eventually climb gently and reach a minor road. Turn right to follow this quiet road downhill, eventually emerging on the main road just east of Evanton. Turn right, crossing the river and passing the caravan site and the Novar Arms to return to the village centre.

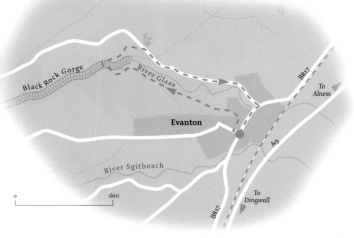

Fyrish Monument

Distance **6km** Time **2 hours**
Terrain **good woodland path with a fair
bit of up and down** Map **OS Explorer 438**
Access **no public transport to start**

The great monument atop Cnoc Fyrish
is a prominent landmark for miles
around and a compelling challenge
to those who like to explore on foot.
The waymarked walk to visit its
distinctive arches gives memorable
views over the Cromarty Firth.

The walk begins from a dedicated car
park on the left side of the minor road
from Alness to Boath. The route to the
monument is signposted as the Jubilee
Path and begins by heading through the
gate and into the forest. The path rises and

falls gently at first; go straight across at a
forestry track. Further on, descend a flight
of stone steps to cross a footbridge over a
burn. At another junction go straight
ahead once more (waymarker post).

Eventually the path begins to climb
clear of the tree cover, revealing stunning
views back towards Alness and over the
Cromarty Firth and the Black Isle. At a
crossroads there is a sign indicating a
track off to the right – this makes an
alternative route for the return; for now
continue straight ahead once more, across
more open moorland.

The monument is reached about half a
kilometre further on. It is even more
impressive in close-up than when seen
from the A9 far below – a huge structure

consisting of three central arches and four further flanking towers. It was built in 1783 by the local laird, Sir Hector Munro, once the commander of British Forces in India. Sir Hector had defeated the Dutch at the Battle of Negapatam before eventually returning to the Highlands. This was at the time of the Clearances and there was much suffering and even starvation in the area. Famine relief was usually provided only in return for work – it being feared that feeding the starving would make them lazy – and the construction of the monument was one of the tasks given to the local destitute. It is said to be a replica of the gates of Negapatam; a memorial to Sir Hector's great victories. For today's walkers there are other rewards as the

views from the monument are tremendous, with the whole sweep of the Cromarty Firth below, whilst out to the west the view is dominated by the great bulk of Ben Wyvis.

The descent is best made the same way. It is possible to vary the route slightly from the crossroads just beyond a lochan where a signpost indicates the alternative turn-off to the left. This track leads down to a T-junction; from here a right turn (waymarked) eventually regains the outward route further on. Turn left here to retrace your steps to the car park.

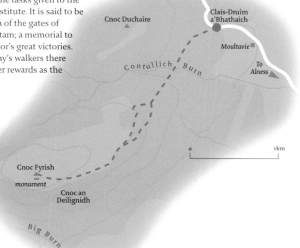

Cnoc Duchaire

Clais-Druim a'Bhathaich

Moultavie

To Alness

Contullich Burn

0   1km

Cnoc Fyrish

monument

Cnoc an Deilignidh

Big Burn

◀ Fyrish Monument overlooking the Cromarty Firth

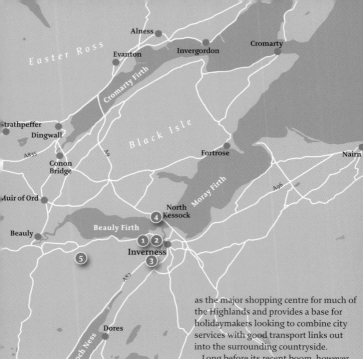

Inverness has long been the capital and administrative centre of the Highlands, and in 2001 it became Scotland's newest city. Recently it has become home to government agencies, new hi-tech businesses and one of the campuses for the University of the Highlands and Islands; it is reckoned to be one of Europe's fastest growing cities. It also acts as the major shopping centre for much of the Highlands and provides a base for holidaymakers looking to combine city services with good transport links out into the surrounding countryside.

Long before its recent boom, however, Inverness was an important settlement. Strategically sited on the Moray Firth at the head of the Great Glen, it was once a Pictish stronghold, possibly based on Craig Phadrig. St Columba is said to have visited in 565AD to convert King Brude to Christianity. More than a thousand years later, in 1745, the Battle of Culloden took place just east of the city; repercussions from the brutal suppression of the people of the Highlands and their culture which followed were felt for centuries.

Inverness Castle ▶

Inverness

Craig Phadrig

Distance **2km** Time **1 hour**
Terrain **waymarked woodland paths; steep in places, sometimes muddy**
Map **OS Explorer 416** Access **Kinmylies bus (8) from Inverness Bus Station to Leachkin Road/Leachkin Brae junction**

Visit the site of the ancient fort of Craig Phadrig for great views over the City of Inverness and across the Beauly Firth.

There is parking at the start of this walk, reached from the centre of Inverness by taking the A862 Beauly road as far as the Caledonian Canal. Once over the canal, turn left onto Leachkin road at the traffic lights, then fork right onto Leachkin Brae (SP Craig Phadrig Forest Walk). After a short, steep climb the

car park is reached on the right.

Craig Phadrig can claim to be the spot where the City of Inverness was founded. It is thought that sometime between 400 and 600AD this hill was the base for the Pictish ruler, King Brude. According to folklore this is where St Columba came when he arrived in Scotland on a mission to convert the Picts to Christianity. At first Brude denied entry to the Irish missionary, but the gates to his fortress opened spontaneously in front of Columba. On witnessing this miracle Brude converted to Christianity along with his people.

From the car park, pass the Forestry Commission sign and head into the trees. Take the first fork on the right (just before

◂ The Beauly Firth from the top of Craig Phradrig

the main path rises to meet a track) and descend before climbing uphill for a short distance. Branch right at the next fork following the yellow waymarker and keeping an eye out for the next path on the right marked in blue. Take this path as it climbs through the trees, staying on the main path.

When the ground levels off slightly, below a steep final section, detour up a the path on the left to visit the site of the iron-age fort. The summit is grassy and you can make out the outline of the double wall of the oval fortress, thought to date from around 500BC. Archaeologists believe the walls would once have stood at least 8m in height, and excavations in the 1970s revealed that many of the stones in the walls had been vitrified – fused together using very high temperatures, in a similar way to other ancient strongholds in the area.

The strategic importance is immediately apparent as you head around the rim of the fort with its expansive views over the Beauly Firth to Ben Wyvis and, despite being partly obscured by trees, a good view down over Inverness. At the far end of the summit, a narrow path descends steeply. Follow this straight down to soon rejoin the original path as it heads around the hill. Turn left onto this and left again at the next junction, following yellow waymarkers. Keep on the yellow trail passing some houses with panoramic views on a track before turning left onto a clear marked path which returns to the car park.

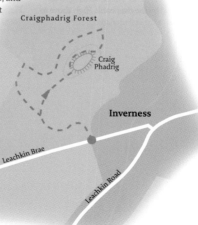

Waterways of Inverness

Distance 11.5km **Time** 4 hours
Terrain canal towpath, riverside path,
roads with pavements
Map OS Explorer 416 **Access** Inverness is
well served by buses and trains

**Inverness is lucky to have two very
attractive waterways passing through it;
this half-day walk around the city explores
both the River Ness and the Caledonian
Canal as well as taking in some of the
shoreline of the Beauly Firth.**

Start from the tourist information centre
on Bridge Street (the lower end of the High
Street) in the centre of Inverness. Head
down to the river but turn left along the
near side on Castle Street, sticking to the
pavement by the river bank. High above to
the left are the red sandstone walls of
Inverness Castle, currently used as a

courthouse. The castle seen today only
dates back to 1836 although there have been
fortresses on this imposing site since the
11th century. Keep right when the road forks
to continue by the river, passing but not
crossing a pedestrian suspension bridge.

Pass the war memorial and continue
until a bridge gives you access to the first of
the Ness Islands. Follow the path as it
crosses to the next island before heading
over a suspension bridge to reach the far
side of the river. You are now on the Great
Glen Way, a long-distance walking route
which links Inverness with Fort William.

Turn left on the far side of the river and
turn right (SP Great Glen Way) up a road
which passes the leisure centre and the
Floral Hall, whose welcoming greenhouses
are recommended on a chilly day. At the
main road beyond cross carefully and turn

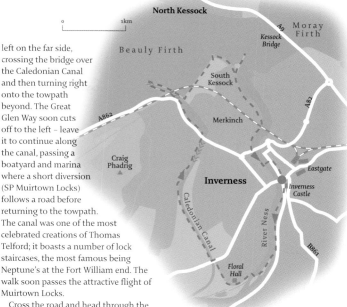

left on the far side, crossing the bridge over the Caledonian Canal and then turning right onto the towpath beyond. The Great Glen Way soon cuts off to the left – leave it to continue along the canal, passing a boatyard and marina where a short diversion (SP Muirtown Locks) follows a road before returning to the towpath. The canal was one of the most celebrated creations of Thomas Telford; it boasts a number of lock staircases, the most famous being Neptune's at the Fort William end. The walk soon passes the attractive flight of Muirtown Locks.

Cross the road and head through the iron gate to continue by the canal, eventually heading over the railway before reaching the final lock at Clachnaharry. Here the canal meets the waters of the Beauly Firth, its coast to coast journey complete. Cross over the lock near the end and head back up the far bank, crossing the railway line once more. Turn left (SP Old Ferry Pier and South Kessock) to the seawall which is a good spot for watching wading birds. A third crossing of the railway brings you to a gate into a picnic area at South Kessock. The Moray Firth

dolphins are sometimes sighted from here, whilst the shoreline is a haunt of otters. Follow the road in front of the houses with good views of the Kessock Bridge ahead. The route now passes through a more industrial area; branch left at a fork after the plumbing centre to follow the road next to the river, passing under the rail tracks and following the more residential Gilbert Street. Remain on the river bank until a pedestrian suspension bridge; cross this and turn right to return to the start.

◀ Greig Street Bridge spanning the River Ness

Caledonian Canal to Dochgarroch Lock

Distance 12km **Time** 3 hours 30
Terrain level canal towpath
Map OS Explorer 416 **Access** Inverness is
well served by buses and trains

**Follow the Caledonian Canal towpath
from Inverness to the locks at
Dochgarroch near Loch Ness and return on
the far side and watch the water-borne
activities of man and wildlife.**

This walk starts from Whin Park on the
banks of the River Ness, near the leisure
centre on the west side of Inverness. You
can either walk here from the city centre by
following the River Ness upstream,
crossing at the Ness Islands, or if driving
follow the A82 signed for Drumnadrochit
and, just before the bridge over the canal,
turn left to reach the small car park and
toilets at Whin Park on the right-hand side.

From here continue upstream on the
riverside path, crossing a footbridge; in a
short while wooden steps lead to the
towpath of the Caledonian Canal. Bear left
along the towpath which forms a barrier
between the river on the left and the canal.
Even today the canal, which joins the west
and east coasts of Scotland, is an amazing
feat of engineering. Following a natural
fault across the Highlands it links the
lochs in the Great Glen, most notably Loch
Ness, by a series of extra-wide channels
and locks built to accommodate large
steamships. The canal was the brainchild
of Thomas Telford, who was not only
passionate about design and building but
also wanted to breath new economic life
into a Highlands impoverished by the twin
evils of the potato famine and the
Highland Clearances. Echoing the

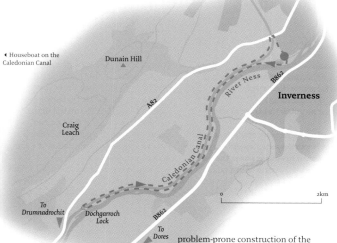

◀ Houseboat on the
Caledonian Canal

Dunain Hill

Craig
Leach

Inverness

Caledonian Canal

River Ness

A82

B862

To
Drumnadrochit

Dochgarroch
Lock

B862

To
Dores

0   2km

problems encountered by modern-day
large-scale schemes, the project ran over
budget and over time. Eventually it was
completed 12 years later than expected, in
1822, with the original design narrowed to
save costs. By this time iron construction
was allowing larger and larger boats to be
built, many of which were too big to pass
through the canal. Combined with the
development of the railways, the
Caledonian Canal never realised its
potential to carry commercial traffic,
although it has since become a popular
tourist attraction and leisure boat route.

Keep following the towpath and after
5km the locks at Dochgarroch are reached.
This is a popular mooring for boats of all
shapes and sizes. It was here that the

problem-prone construction of the
canal was hit by a minor earthquake in
1901 which left a a half-inch wide crack
running along the towpath for 600 metres.
Cross the canal at the lock (just up towards
the road is a tearoom and antique shop)
and head back towards Inverness on the
far bank.

The towpath passes several buildings
and at one point the main track heads left
away from the canal; here, stay on the
smaller canalside path. Nearer to Inverness
the route passes some houses and the
end of a small road before reaching
Tomnahurich Swing Bridge which carries
the main A82 across the canal. Cross this
bridge and then immediately turn right
down the minor road, not the towpath, to
pass behind the leisure centre and the
Floral Hall. This returns you to Whin Park
and the start.

Ord Hill from North Kessock

Distance 4.5km Time 1 hour
Terrain waymarked forest paths and
tracks; gentle climb to top
Map OS Explorer 432
Access no public transport to start

**Guarding the narrows of the Beauly Firth
above North Kessock, Ord Hill is a great
spot to view Inverness across the water.**

This easy walk starts from a car park
accessible only from the southbound
carriageway of the A9 near North Kessock.
To reach it from Inverness, continue to the
next junction for the Black Isle and turn,
when safely off the main road, back down
the south carriageway to the car park on
the left-hand side. Start the walk by
heading up the path at the far southeast
end of the carpark (SP Ord Hill Circular).
Keep straight ahead at the next two
junctions to reach a gate at the edge of the
woods. Pass through and follow the path
as it curves right.

The path traverses the side of the hill; at
a junction the route takes the stepped path
on the left marked with a blue and red
marker, but it is worth making a short
detour ahead for a first view of Inverness.

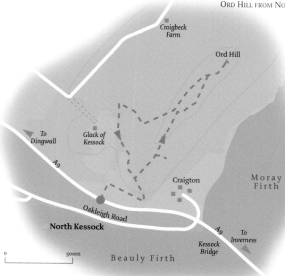

At the top of the steps follow the path to a track, crossing this to climb more steps (SP Viewpoint). At another junction the route continues ahead but by bearing right for a short distance first you reach a superb viewpoint with a bench overlooking Kessock Bridge to Inverness.

The path now climbs through Scots pines, following red waymarkers. Stay on the main path at a junction and follow it to the right, passing a bench. At the next junction turn right to head more steeply uphill. The stones underfoot are the remains of the iron-age vitrified fort which once crowned the summit of the hill. Today the tree cover makes it difficult to make out the outline of the walls of the

stronghold, but the fort once covered the entire summit area.

The highest point of Ord Hill is marked by a stone cairn. From here a circular short path runs around the extent of the fort. Once back at the cairn, initially retrace the outward route, before bearing right at the first junction. Head straight across at the track and aim right at a junction, following the red waymarkers. A few steps lead down to a large track. Follow this straight ahead, soon passing a small parking area. Bear left here (SP North Kessock), eventually passing through a gate and reaching the junction passed earlier in the walk. Branch off to the right to take the path downhill back to the car park.

Kessock Bridge and Inverness from Ord Hill

Reelig Glen

Distance 1.5km **Time** 1 hour
Terrain good woodland paths, picnic area
Map OS Explorer 416 **Access** no public
transport to start

**Magnificent mature trees – including
some of the tallest in Britain – are the
attraction on this pleasant circuit of the
wooded glen alongside the Moniack Burn.**

To reach the car park at the start of this
walk, turn off the A862 west of Inverness
following the sign for Moniack Castle
(worth a visit to sample the locally-made
wines), then keep straight ahead when the
road bends sharply right. From the car park
the walk begins along the wide path which
follows the Moniack Burn upstream.

Much of the local area has been owned
by the Fraser family for most of the past
five centuries. The Frasers had originally
supported the British government during

the Jacobite uprisings of 1715 to 1719 but
later backed the Jacobite cause and many
of the Clan were killed on the front line
during the battles at Falkirk and Culloden.
A member of the next generation, Edward
Satchwell Fraser, fought in the War of
American Independence and one of his five
sons, James Baillie Fraser (1783-1856) was
responsible for planting many of the trees
at Reelig and other parts of the extensive
Fraser estate. Today Reelig Glen is owned
by the Forestry Commission.

Keep following the path, taking either
the steps or the alternative slope, soon
reaching a wooden bridge spanning the
Moniack Burn. This is a modern alternative
to the stone arched bridge seen alongside,
which was built in the 1840s, along with
the stone grotto, as a poor relief scheme
for local tenants displaced by the Highland
Clearances. Keep an eye out for dippers and

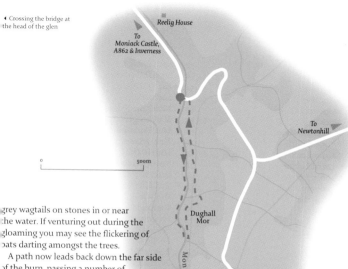

◄ Crossing the bridge at the head of the glen

grey wagtails on stones in or near the water. If venturing out during the gloaming you may see the flickering of bats darting amongst the trees.

A path now leads back down the far side of the burn, passing a number of impressive Douglas fir trees. Among them is the one-time champion of champion trees, Dughall Mor ('big stranger' in Gaelic), which, when last measured in 2009 at 62m high, was Britain's tallest tree. Since then a rival fir growing near Dunans Castle in Argyll has measured even higher and displaced Dughall Mor from the top spot – for the time being anyway as both trees are still thriving.

The path now climbs high above the river, crossing a small footbridge over a tributary and passing a small grotto before descending back down to the Moniack Burn. Cross at the road bridge to return to the car park. From here it is worth making a short detour along the path at the back of the car park (SP Upper Reelig Woodland Walks) to reach a viewpoint nestled amongst mature beech trees. The viewpoint, which overlooks Moniack Castle, actually sits on the site of an iron-age burial mound. You can extend the walk by following any of the paths leading into the higher area of woods but our route returns to the car park at the start.

Index